WORLD'S FAVORITE EASY PIANO PIECES

In Their Original Form

SELECTED
AND
COMPILED BY

MARIE HILL

FOREWORD

In recent years, there has developed a constantly increasing demand for piano music in its original form, showing the styles and forms of eminent composers without distortion or alteration (except for fingering cues and phrasing as an aid to proper interpretation). We previously catered to this demand in two of our World Favorite Series, namely: No. 13 "Classic to Contemporary" and No. 20 "Classics, Old and New" (each presenting early grade piano music in its original form).

In this volume, the accent is on the "popular" rather than the "classic". Many composers, not in the "classic" groups, have written one or more pieces which somehow have attracted the esteem of teachers and students throughout the years and all over the world. Louis Streabbog, for instance, can hardly be called a "classicist", but his easy piano pieces have never been exceeded in popularity in the early grades of instruction. In fact, Streabbog's very effective arrangement of a famous Strauss waltz is included in this collection as a piece in its original form.

This does not imply the exclusion of the masters. The book contains a liberal quantity of great works by Bach, Beethoven, Haydn and others.

In her many years of teaching experience, MARIE HILL has become a leading authority in the choice of piano literature for teaching, recreational and concert purposes. She has written many early grade teaching pieces herself which have gained much popularity, and the publisher has chosen two of them for this book ("Pow Wow" and "Petite Waltz").

Chord names have been inserted above the melody lines of each composition in this book. There is a two-fold value in this: (1) Since the music is of a simple, early grade character, some pupils may want to enrich the harmonies by using full chords in place of single notes or abbreviated chords. (2) The apparent harmonic intent of the composers is more clearly expressed when the simple harmonies fail to clarify this intent. For instance, an E and G combination could be a partial C chord or a short form E minor chord.

We are confident that this volume will provide an important contribution to the field of music appreciation, instruction, and recreation.

CONTENTS

A LITTLE TUNE

LOUIS KOEHLER

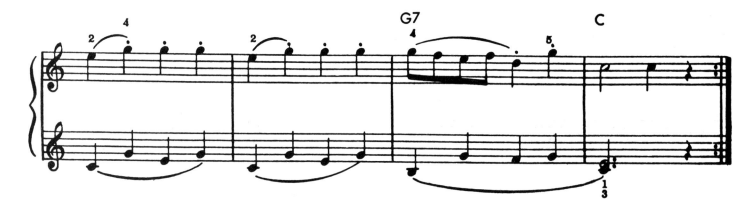

RAINDROPS

JAKOB SCHMITT

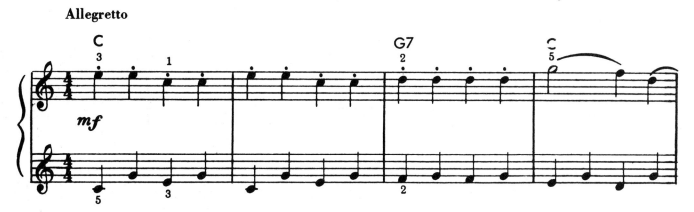

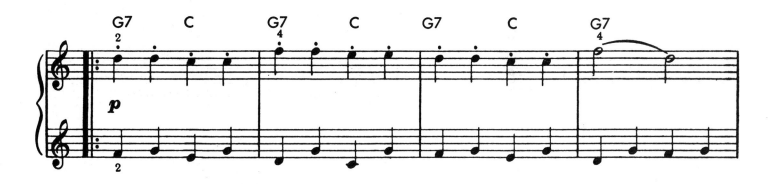

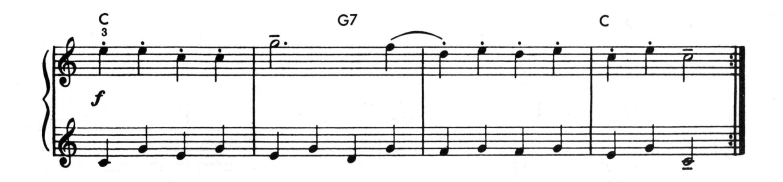

FRENCH CHILD'S SONG

FRANZ BEHR, Opus 575, No. 1

Andantino

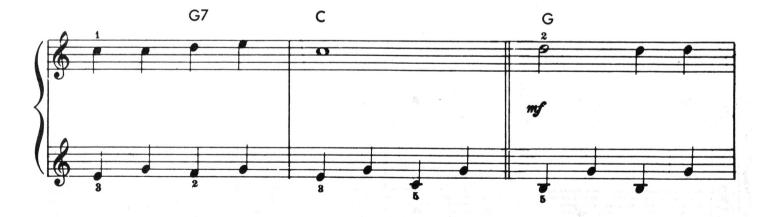

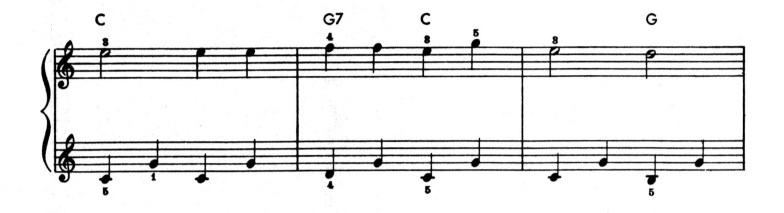

TWINKLE, TWINKLE, LITTLE STAR

FRENCH FOLK TUNE

Moderato

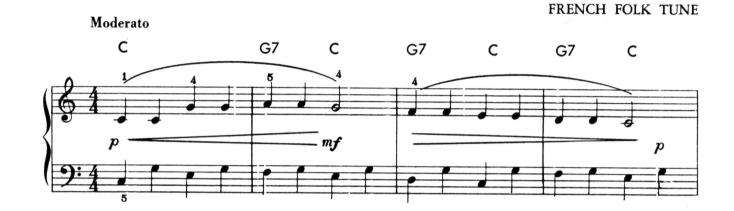

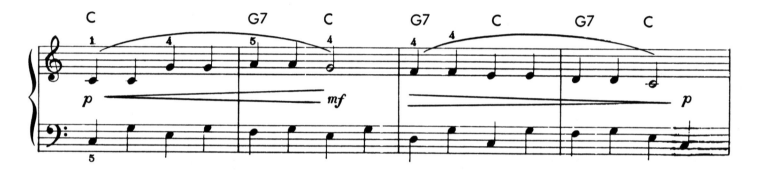

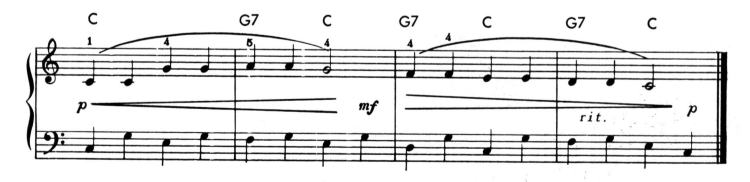

OLD FRENCH AIR

Moderato

FRENCH FOLK TUNE

HUNGARIAN FOLK TUNE

BELA BARTOK

Con brio (forcefully)

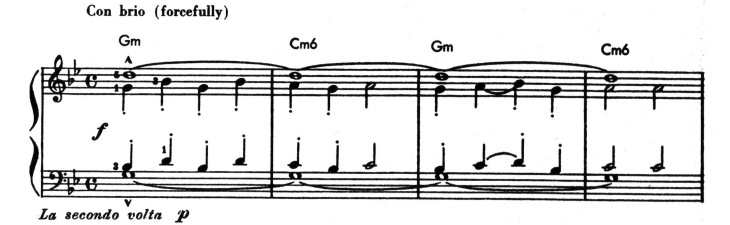

La secondo volta *p*

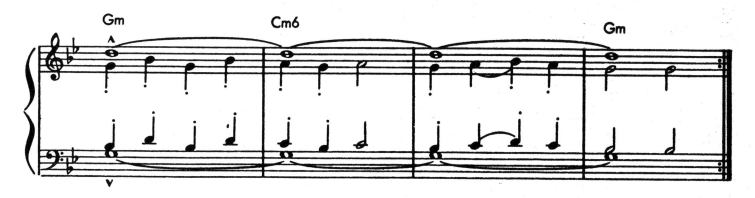

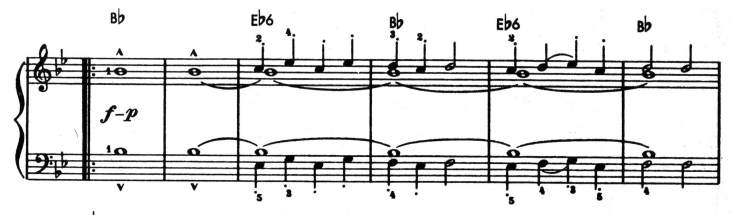

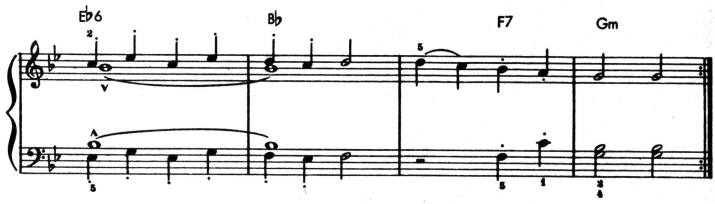

IN UNISON

BELA BARTOK

Moderato

NO CHORDS – ALL IN UNISON

IN THE MONTH OF MAY

FRANZ BEHR, Opus 575, No. 2

Allegretto

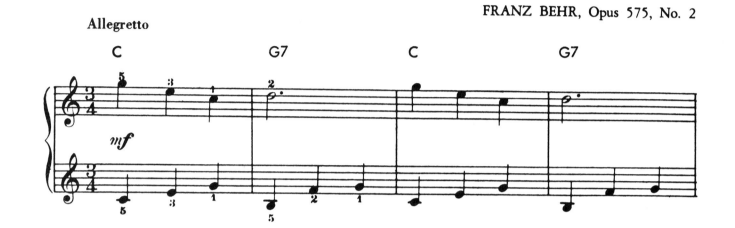

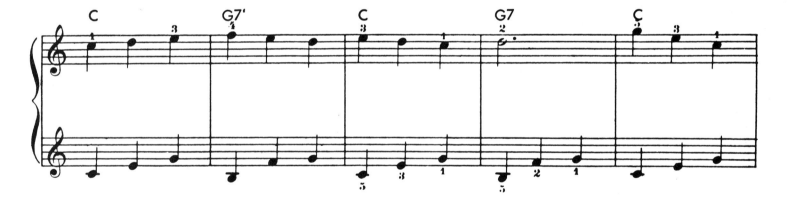

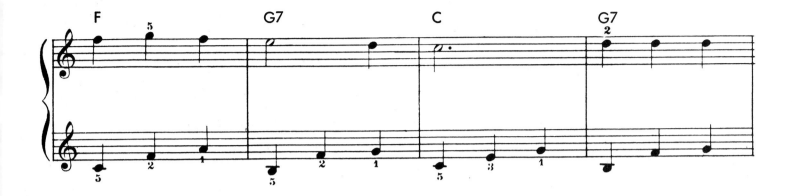

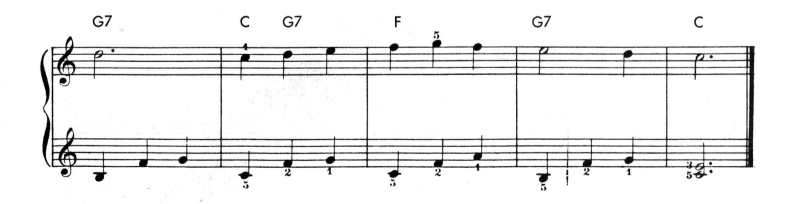

BAGATELLE

ANTONIO DIABELLI

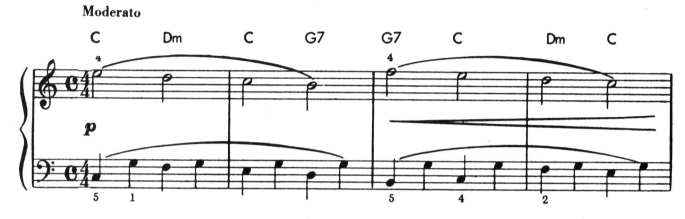

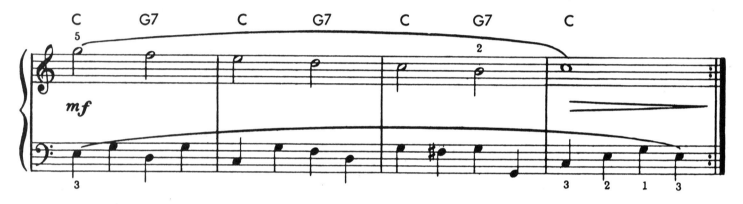

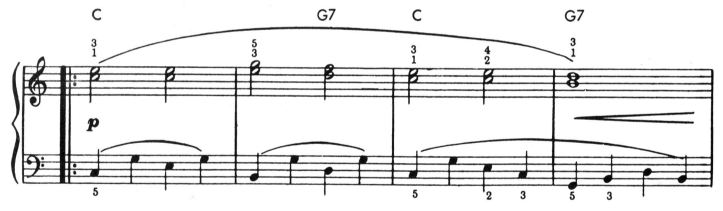

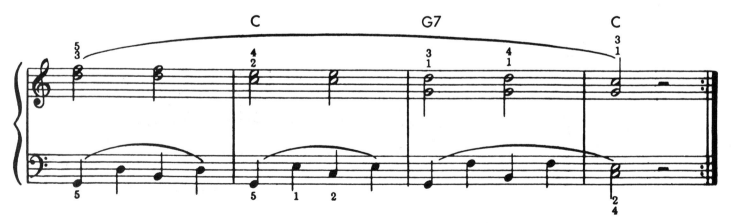

SONATINA IN C

WILLIAM DUNCOMBE

Vivace (lively)

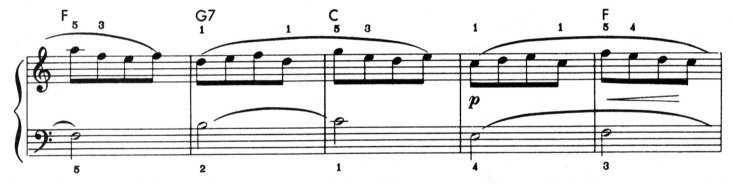

CRADLE SONG

CARL HEINRICH DOERING

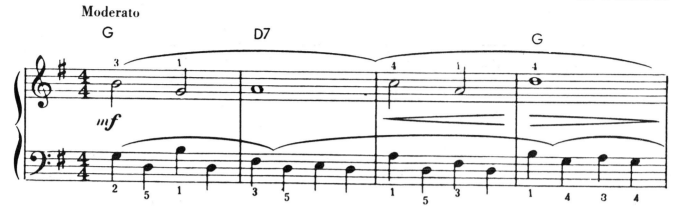

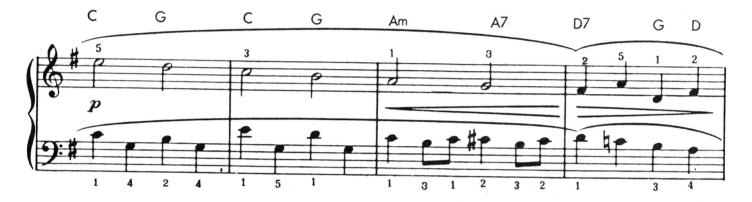

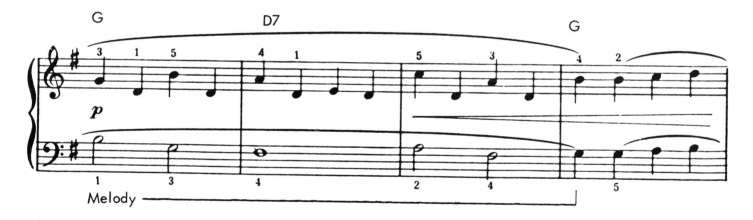

Melody ———

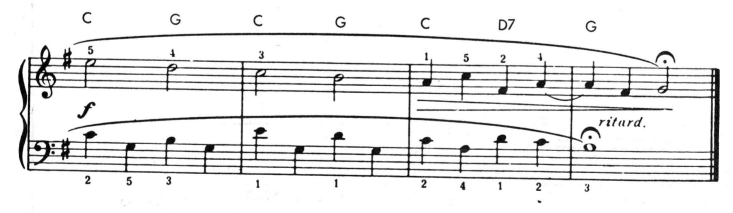

HUNTING SONG

CORNELIUS GURLITT

Allegro

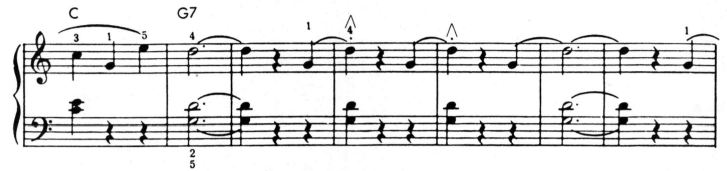

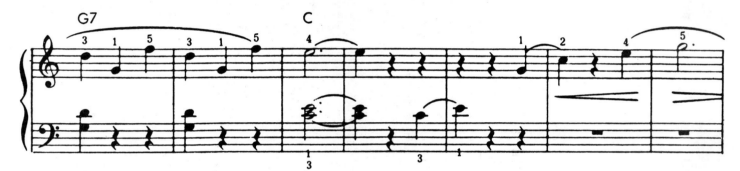

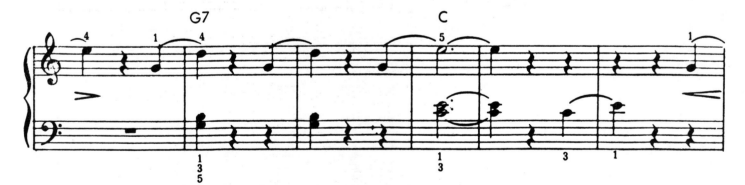

MY CLAVICHORD

FRANZ JOSEF HAYDN

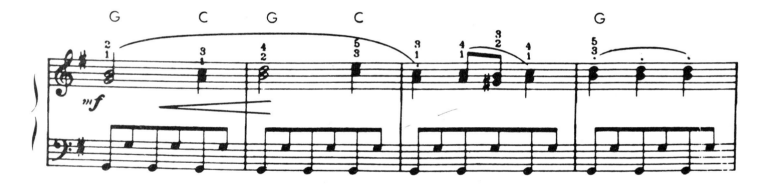

MILADY'S POWDER BOX

Allegretto

FRANZ JOSEF HAYDN

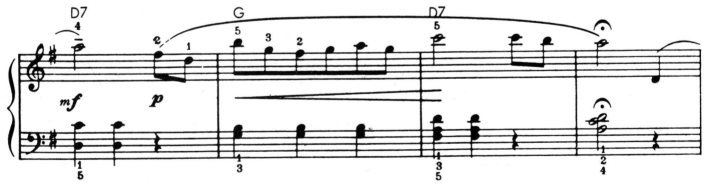

POW WOW

MARIE HILL

Moderato

(Em bass chord throughout the entire piece)

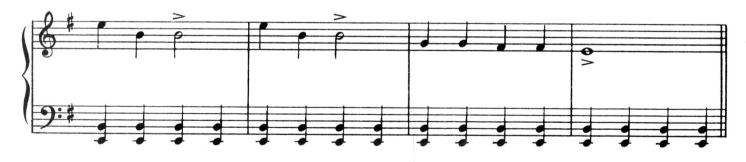

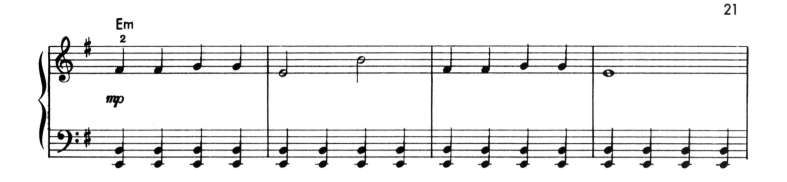

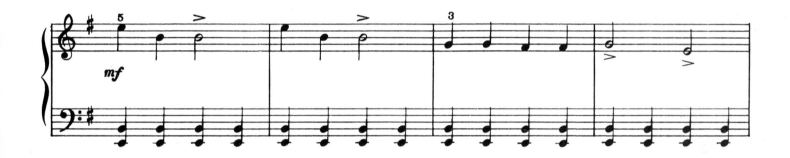

PETITE WALTZ

MARIE HILL

Valse moderato

Dal Segno al Fine

MINUET No. 1
(FROM "ANNA MAGDALENA'S NOTEBOOK")

JOHANN SEBASTIAN BACH

Moderato

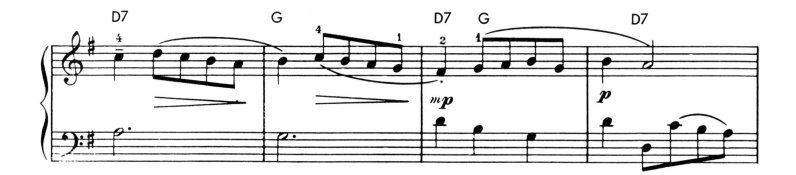

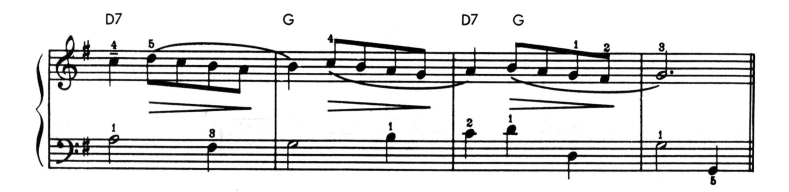

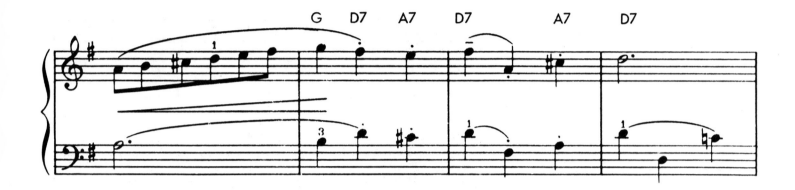

MINUET No. 2
(FROM "ANNA MAGDALENA'S NOTEBOOK")

JOHANN SEBASTIAN BACH

Animato (with spirit)

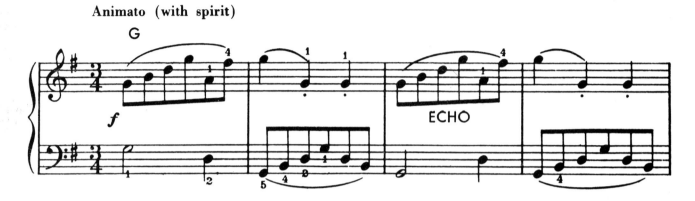

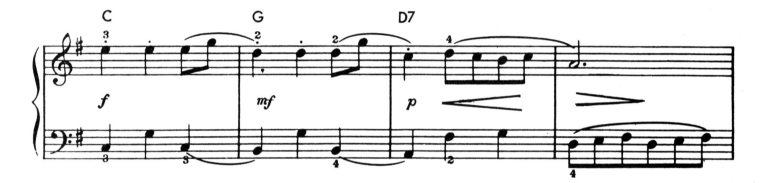

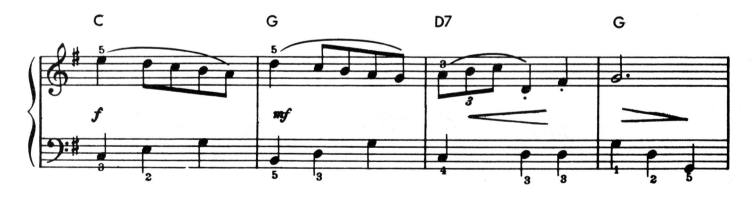

MUSETTE

JOHANN SEBASTIAN BACH

Andante pastorale (calmly)

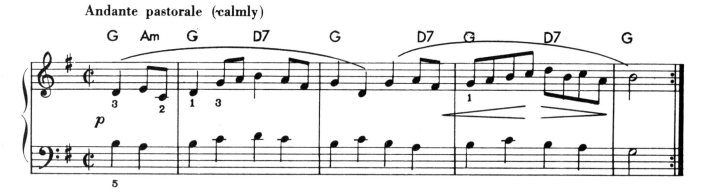

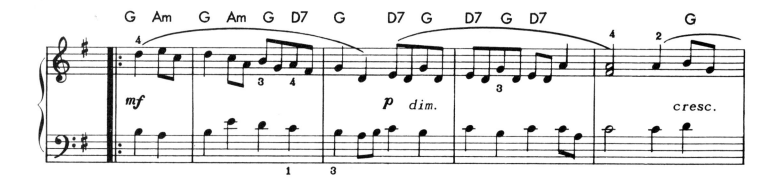

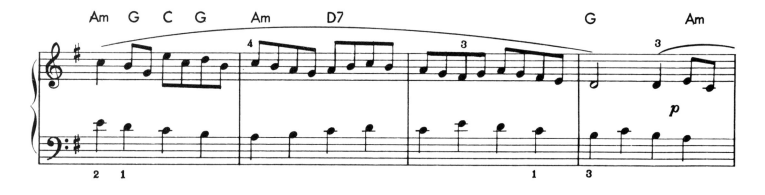

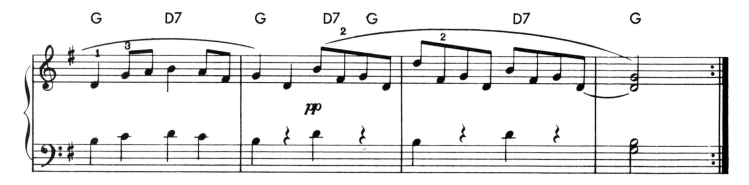

MINUET IN F

JOHANN SEBASTIAN BACH

Andante semplice (simply)

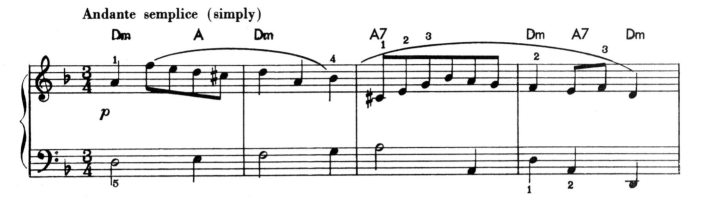

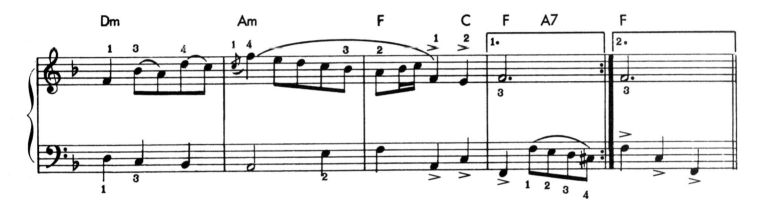

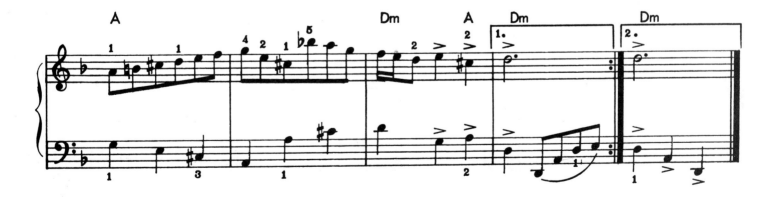

SCHERZO
(FROM "SECOND SONATINA")

FRANZ JOSEF HAYDN

Scherzo (playfully)

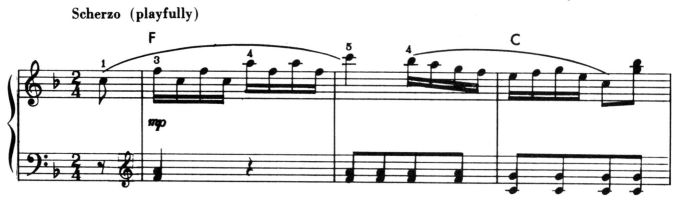

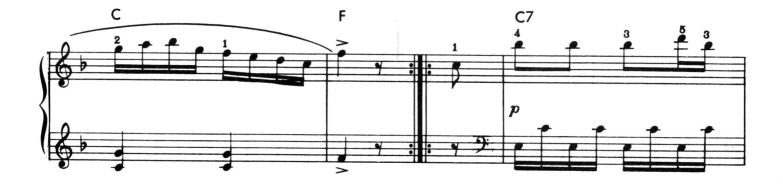

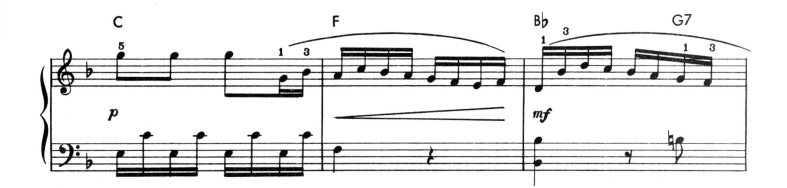

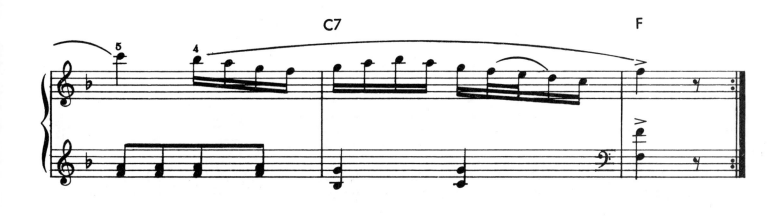

ALLEGRO IN C

CARL CZERNY, Opus 599

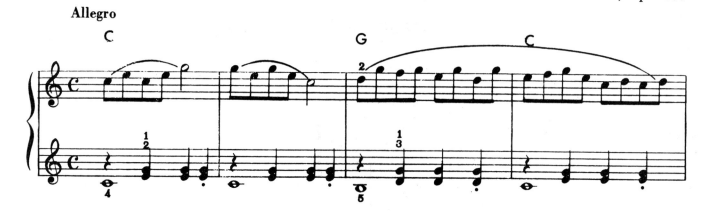

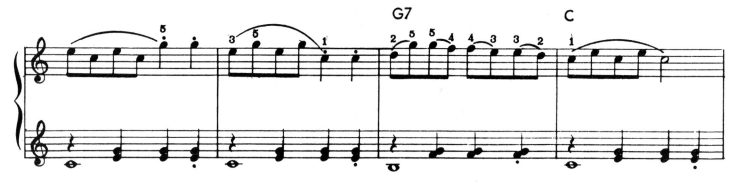

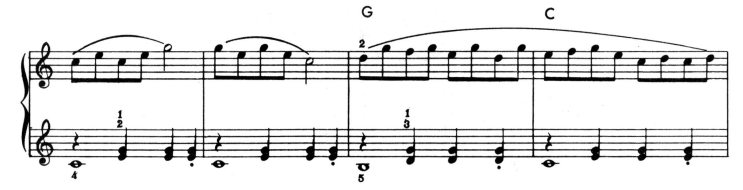

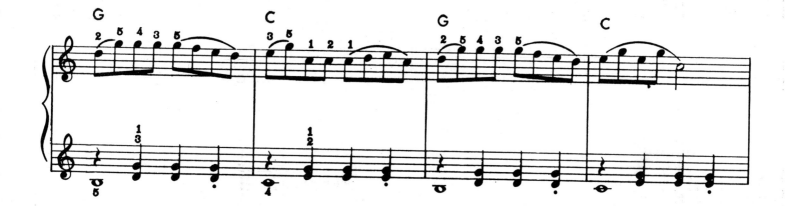

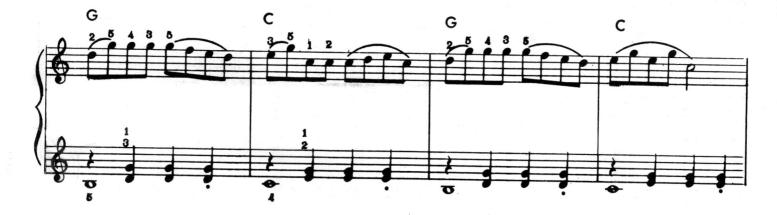

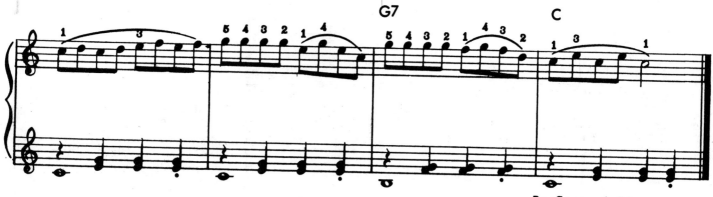

Da Capo al Fine

THE HAREBELL

WILLIAM SMALLWOOD

Moderato

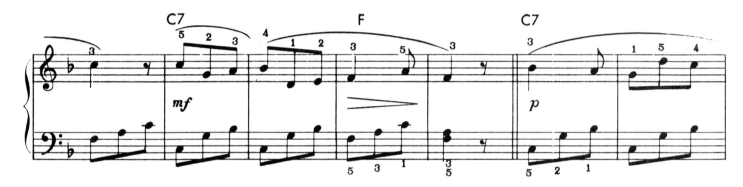

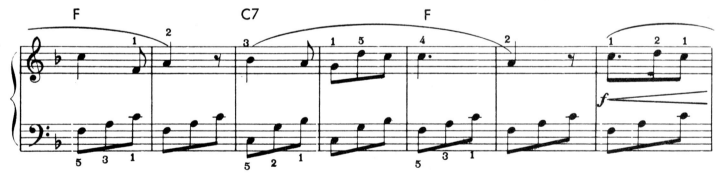

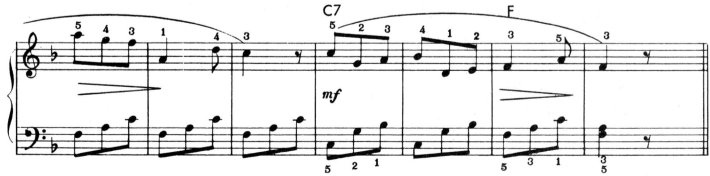

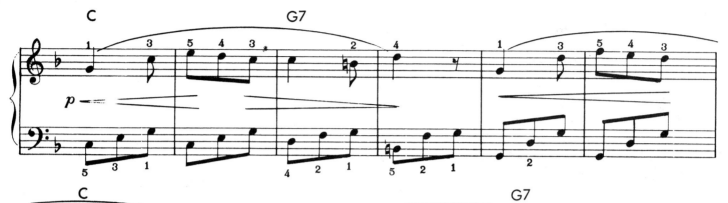

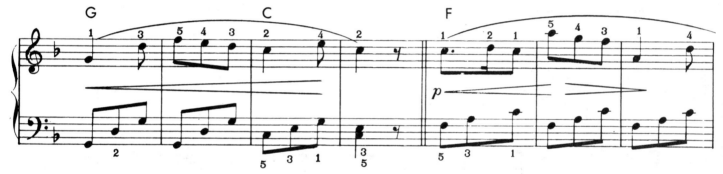

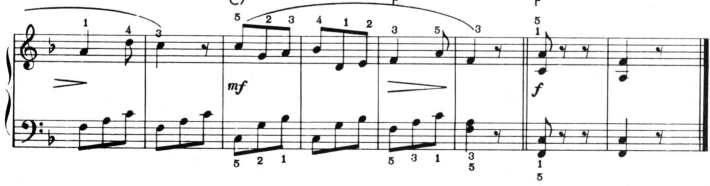

VALSETTE

ALBERT LOESCHHORN

PUPPET WALTZ

HERMAN BERENS

Allegro moderato

THE CRICKET AND THE BUMBLE BEE

GEORGE W. CHADWICK

Allegro moderato

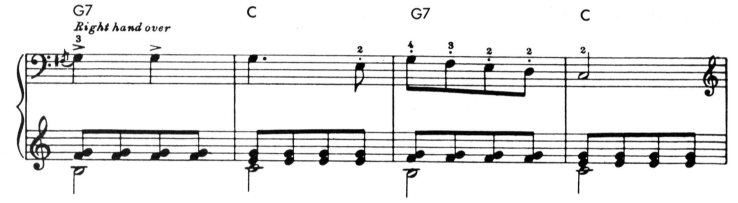

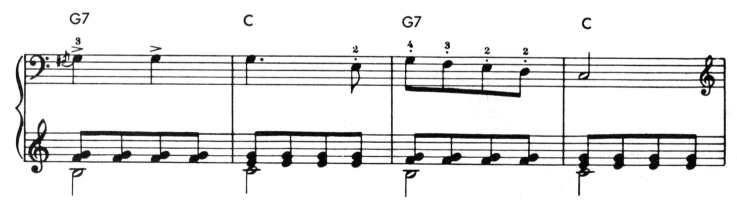

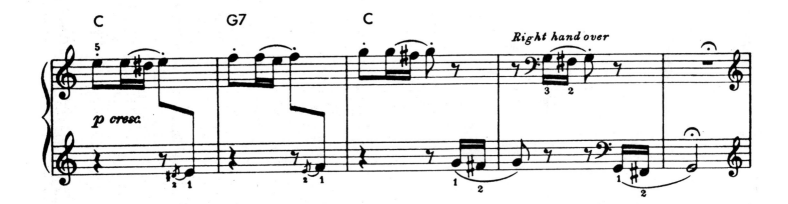

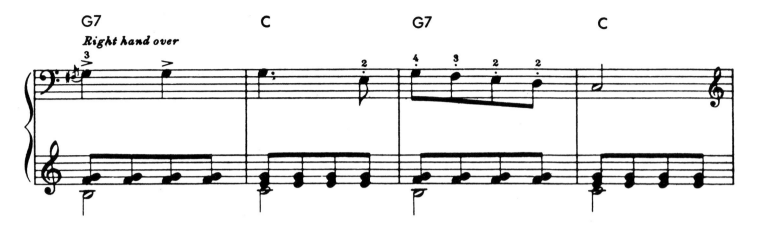

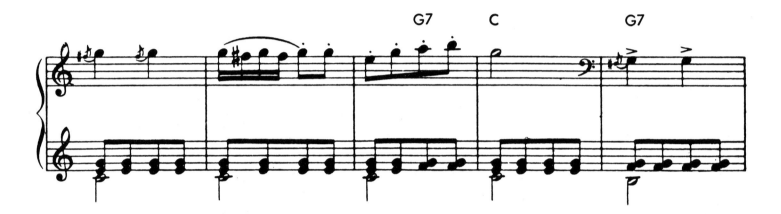

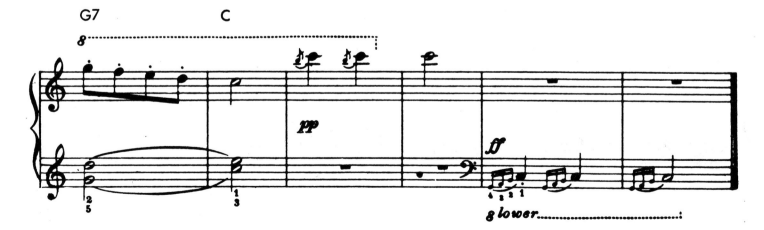

MELODY

DANIEL GOTTLOB TURK

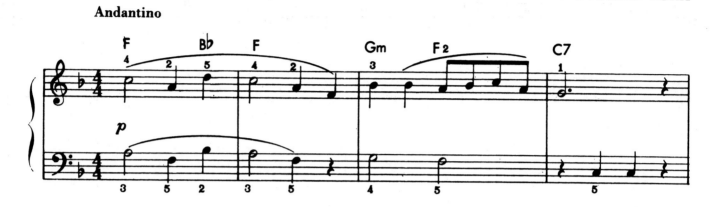

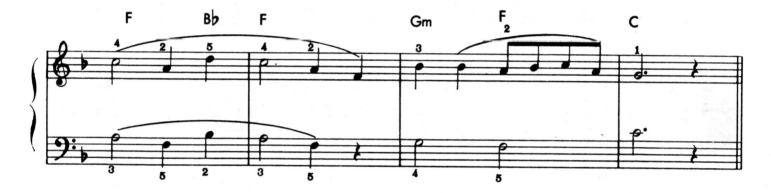

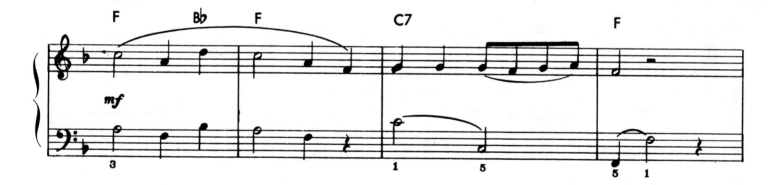

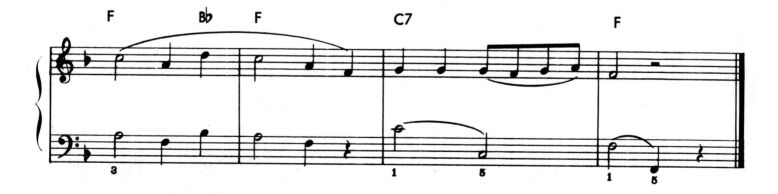

FRISKY GALOP

LOUIS STREABBOG

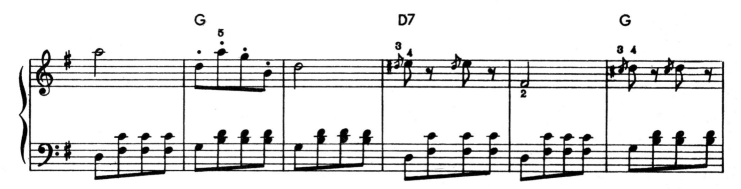

MINNIE WALTZ

LOUIS STREABBOG

Valse moderato

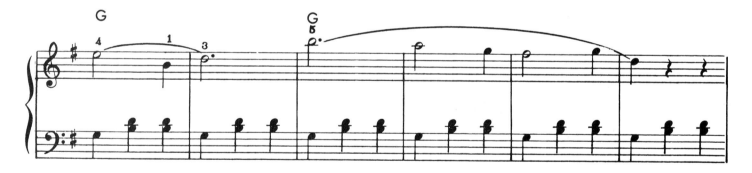

45

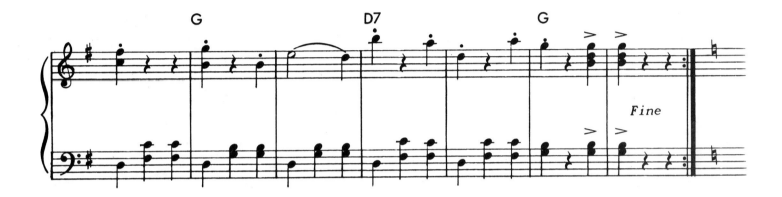

DORA POLKA

LOUIS STREABBORG

Bright polka tempo

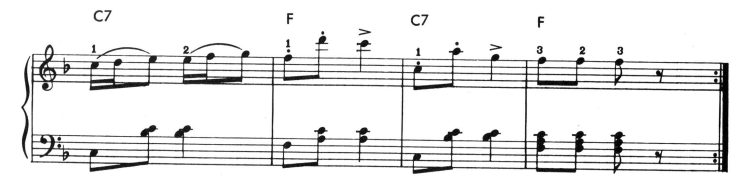

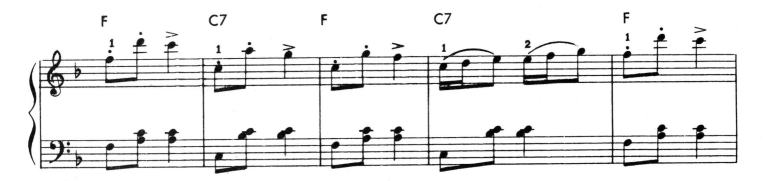

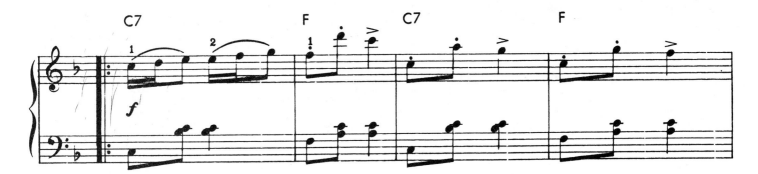

DISTANT BELLS

LOUIS STREABBOG, Opus 64

Andante (slowly)

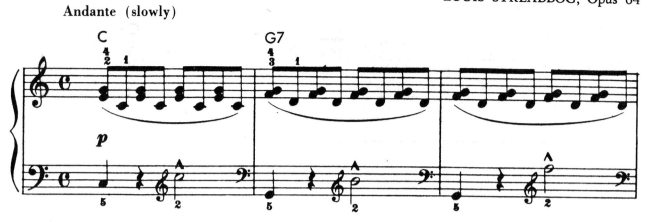

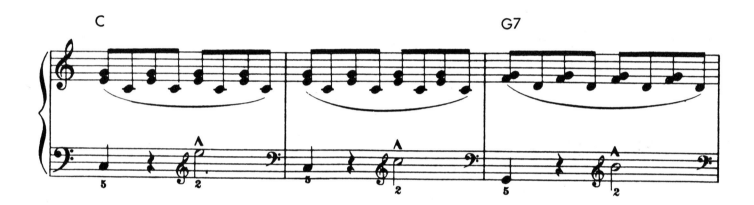

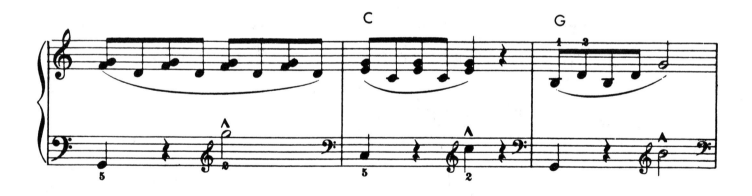

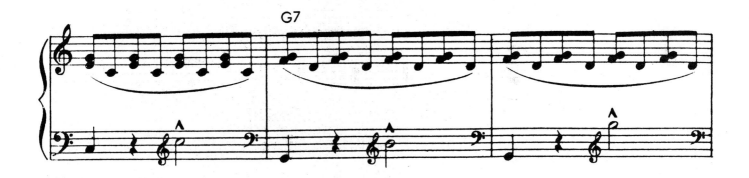

LITTLE FAIRY WALTZ

LOUIS STREABBOG

Valse moderato

p dolce

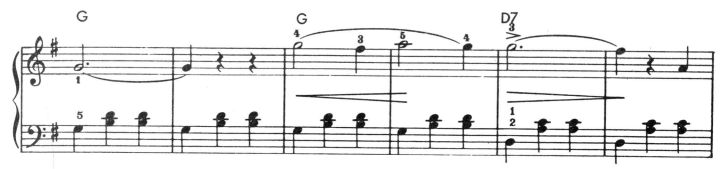

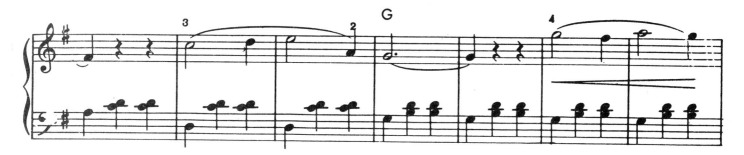

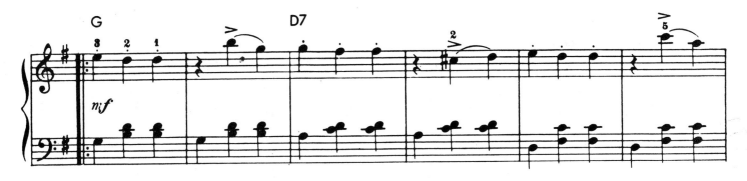

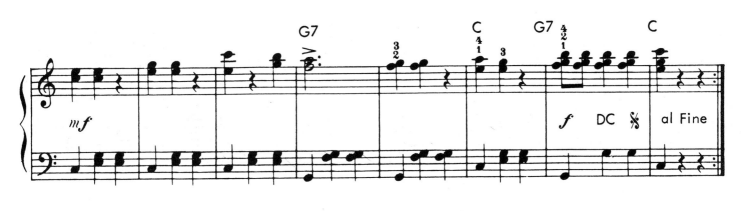

WALTZ

FRANZ BEHR

Valse moderato

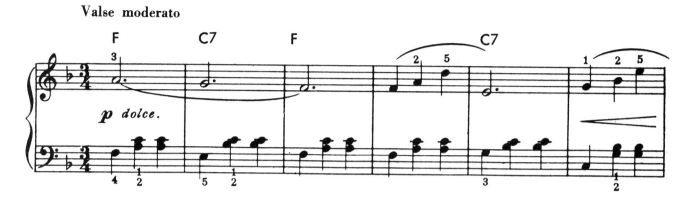

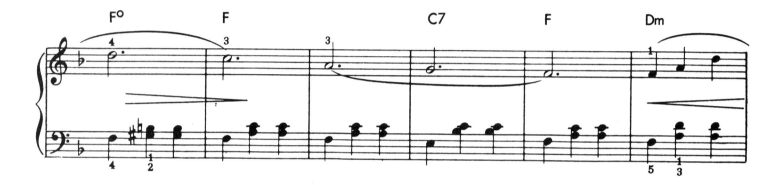

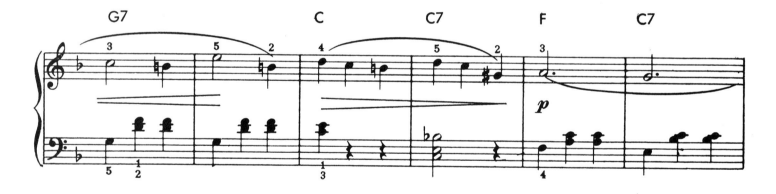

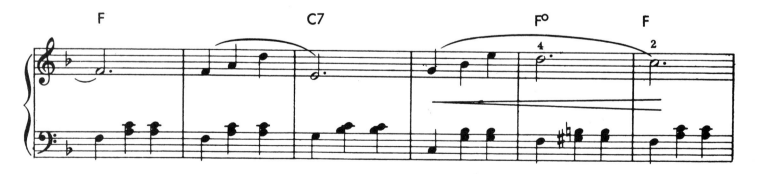

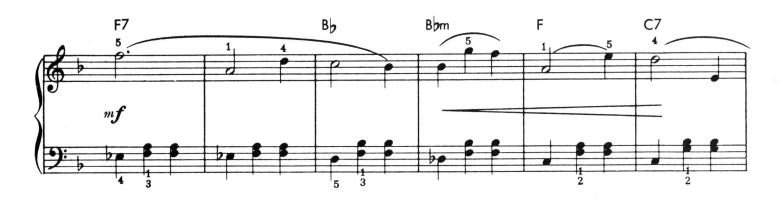

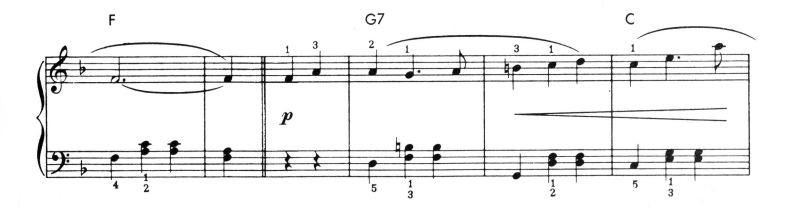

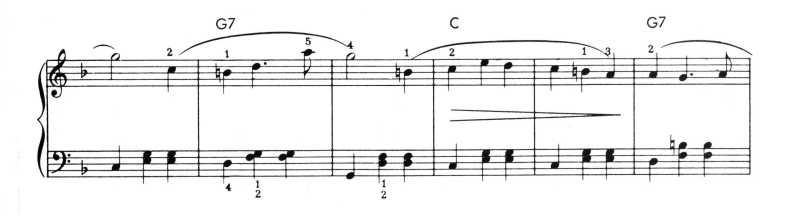

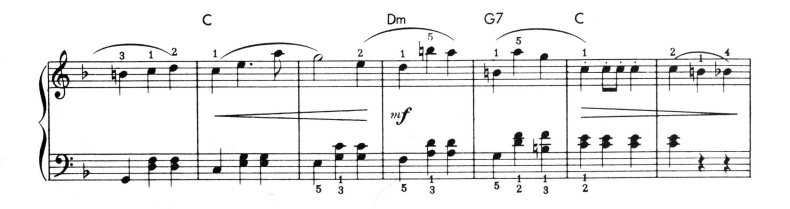

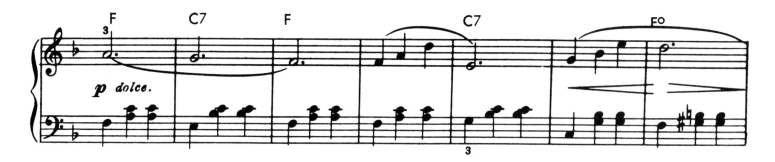

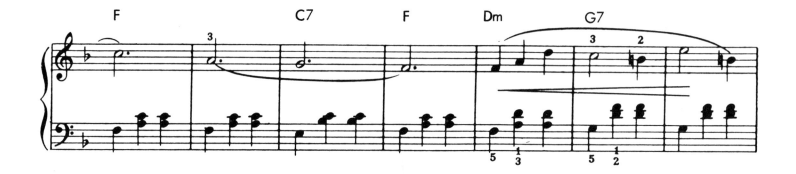

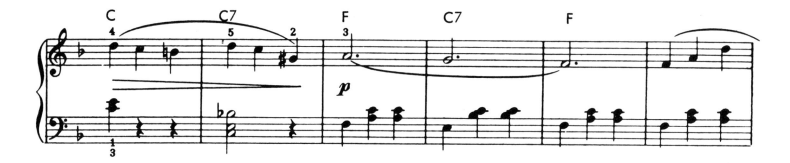

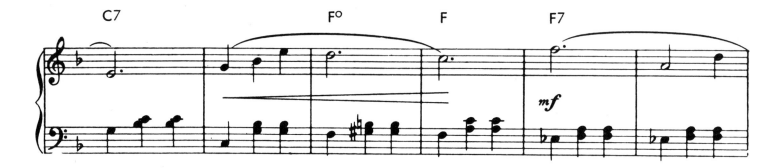

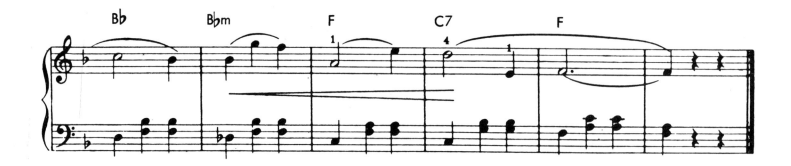

WALTZ IN C

Valse moderato

CORNELIUS GURLITT

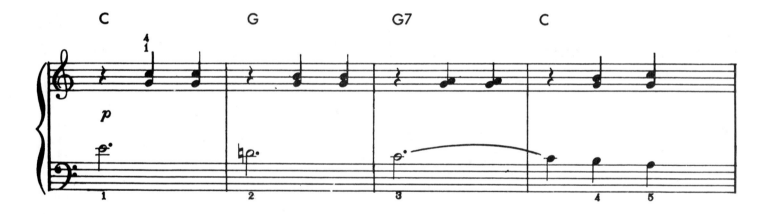

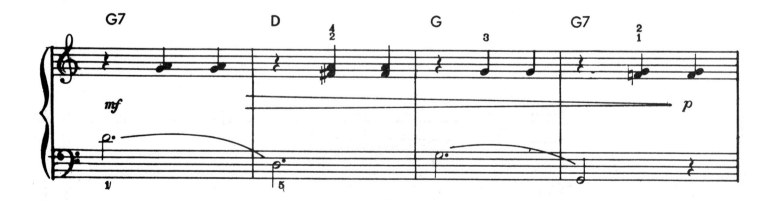

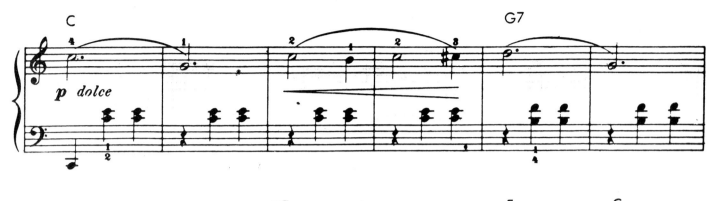

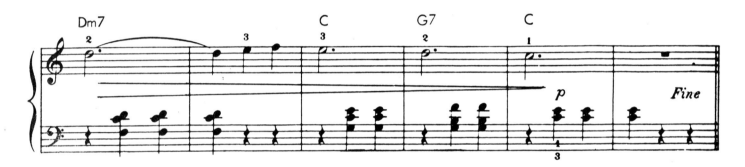

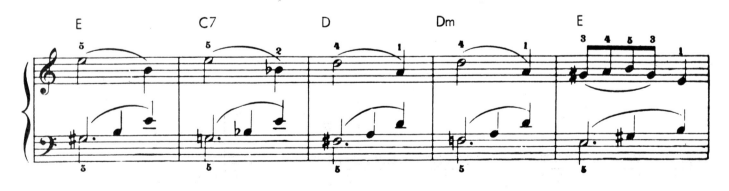

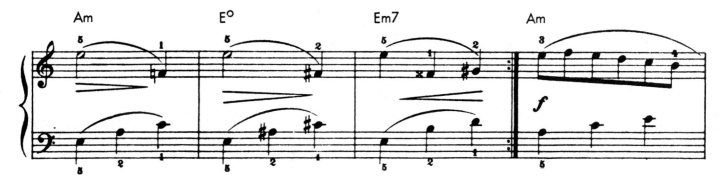

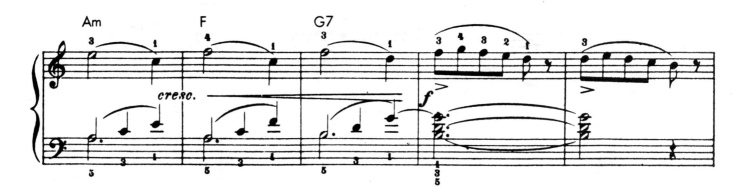

D. C. al Fine

GAVOTTE

CORNELIUS GURLITT

Moderato

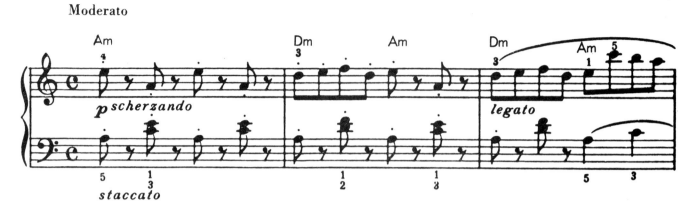

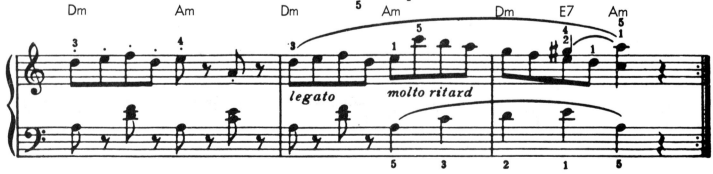

THE FAIR

CORNELIUS GURLITT, Opus 101, No. 8

Vivace (lively)

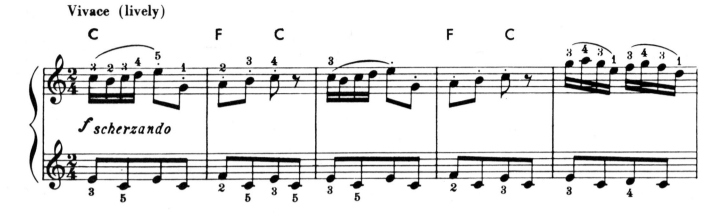

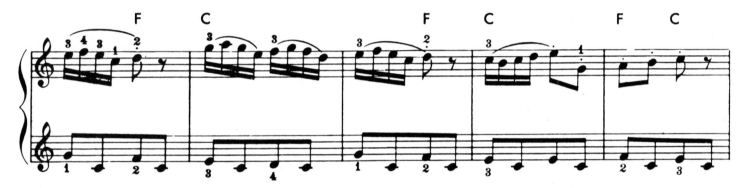

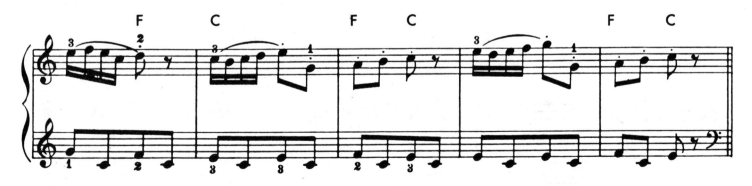

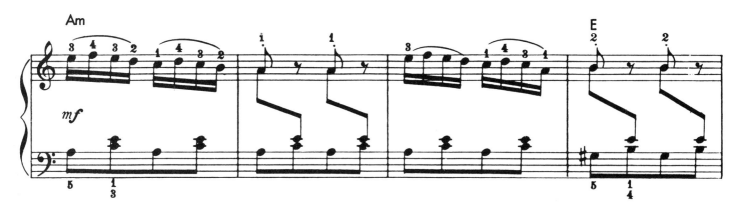

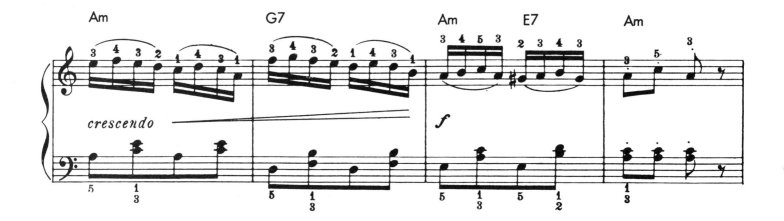

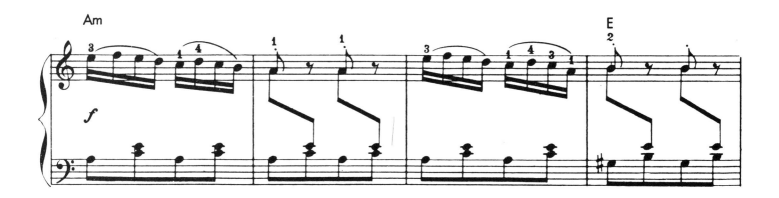

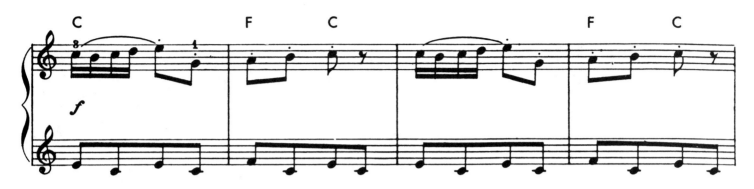

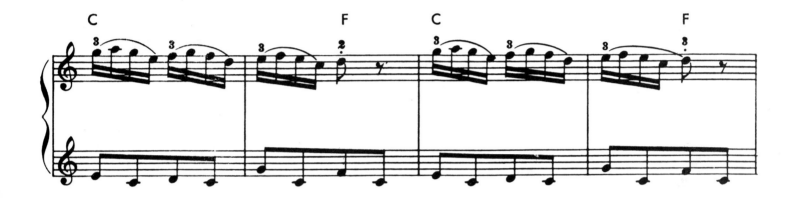

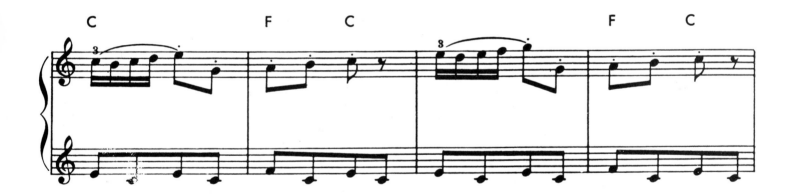

VOICE OF THE HEART

HENRI VAN GAEL, Opus 51

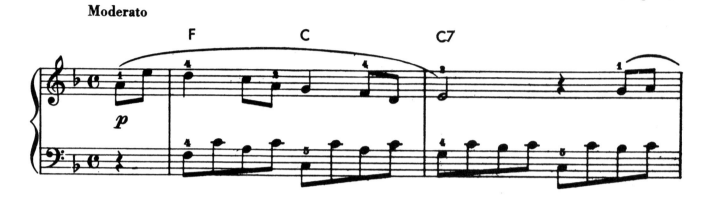

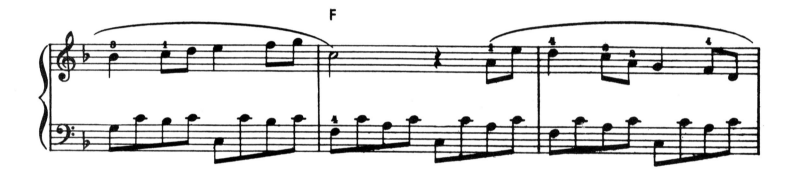

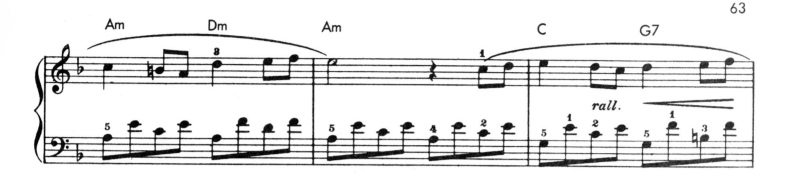

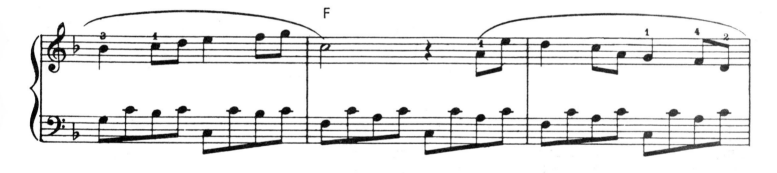

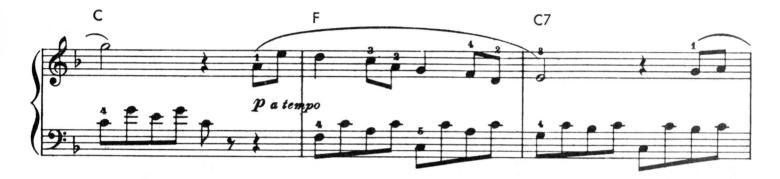

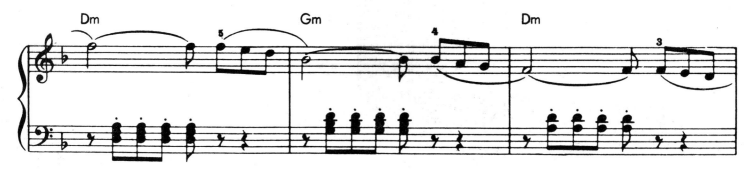

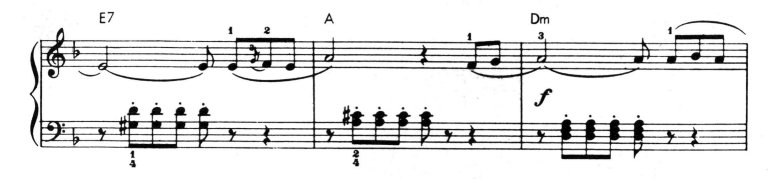

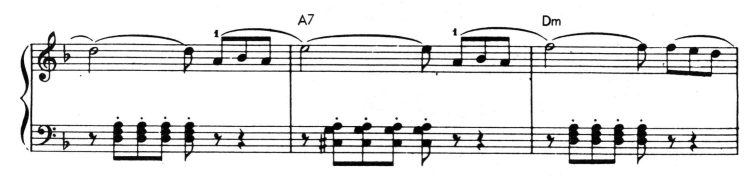

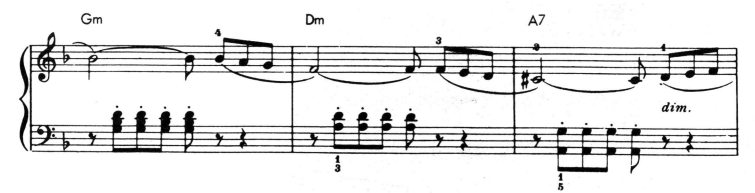

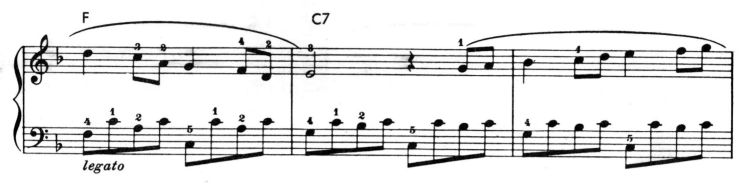

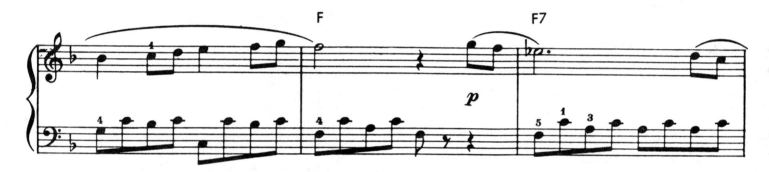

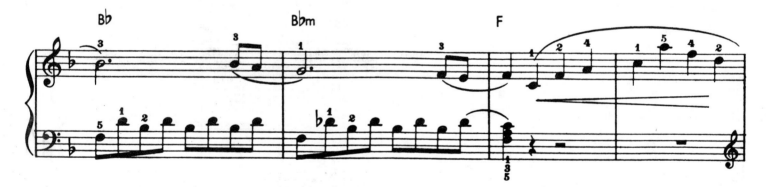

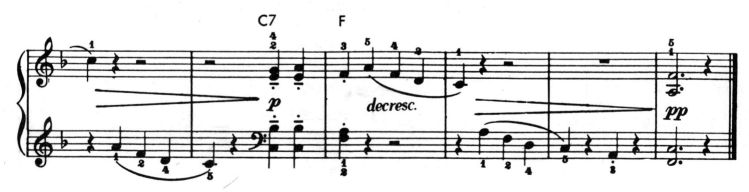

CAMP OF THE GYPSIES

FRANZ BEHR

Allegretto con moto

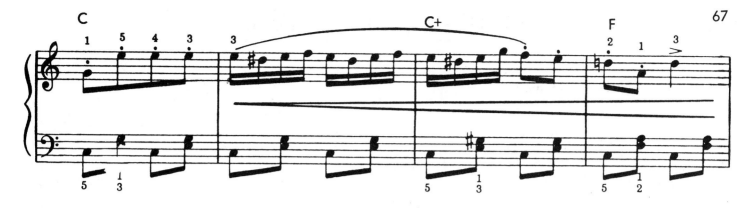

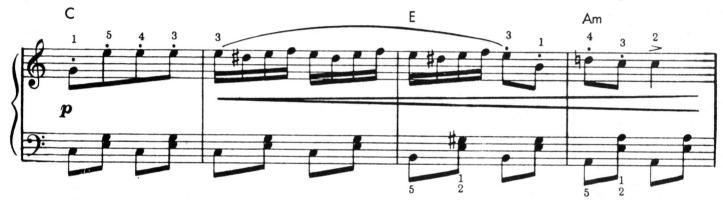

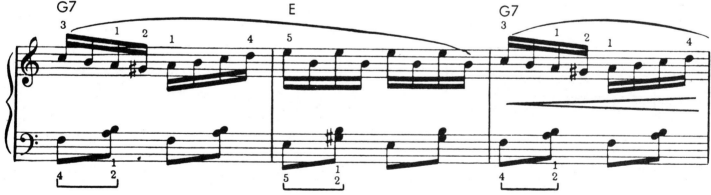

SPINNING SONG

ALBERT ELLMENREICH

Allegretto

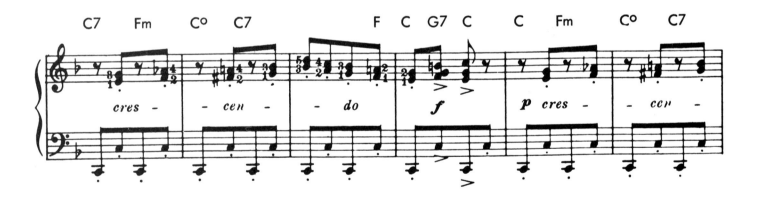

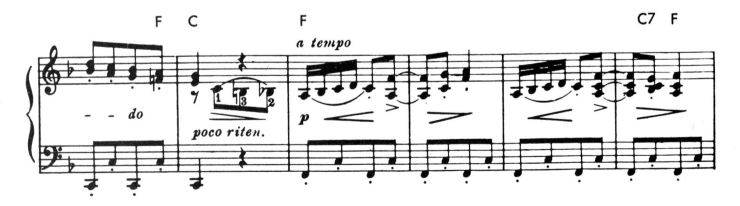

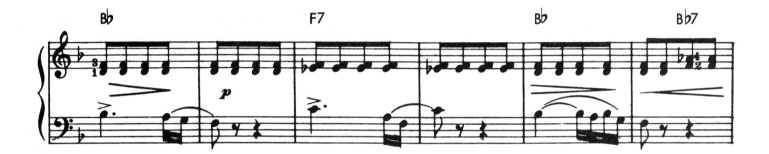

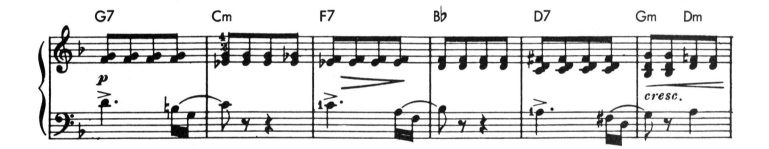

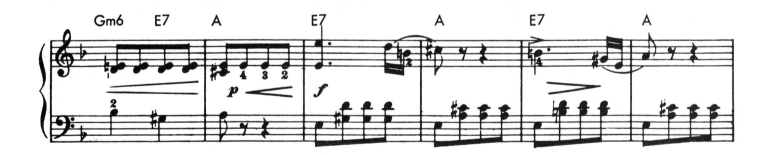

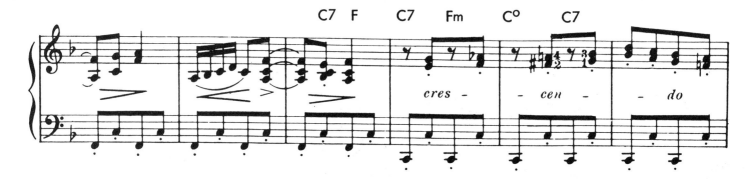

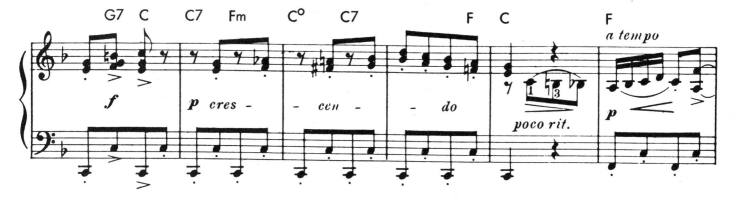

SONATINE

I

JEAN ANTOINE ANDRE

Moderato con moto

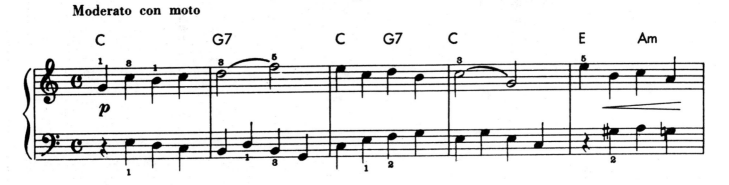

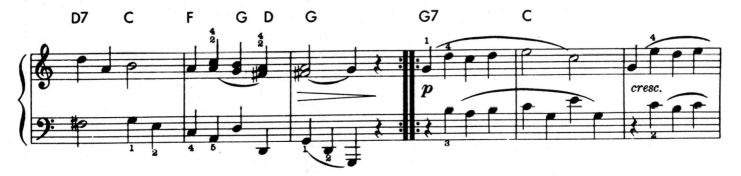

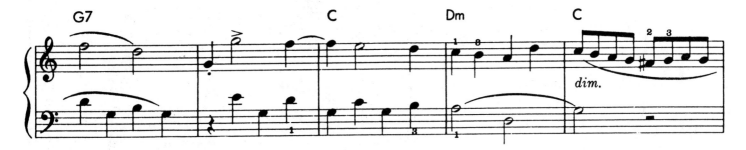

II. Rondo

Allegro

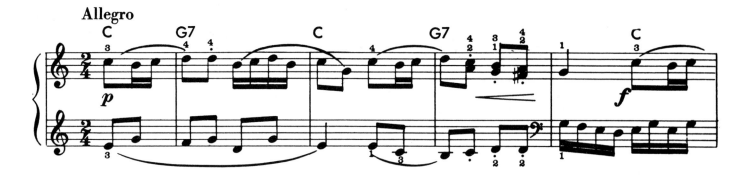

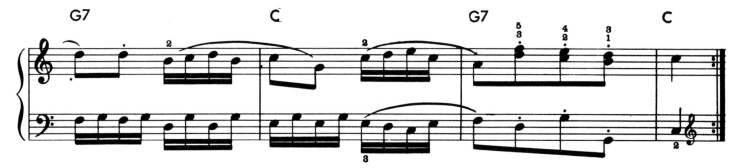

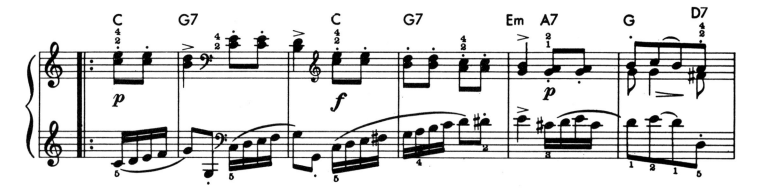

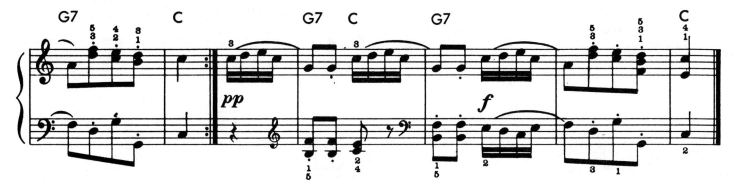

MENUET
(FROM SONATINE IN G)

FRANZ JOSEF HAYDN

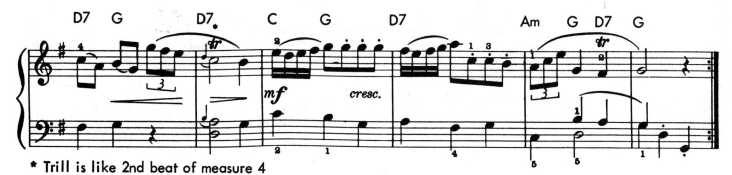

* **Trill is like 2nd beat of measure 4**

ANDANTE

HENRY LOUIS DUVERNOY

Andante (slowly)

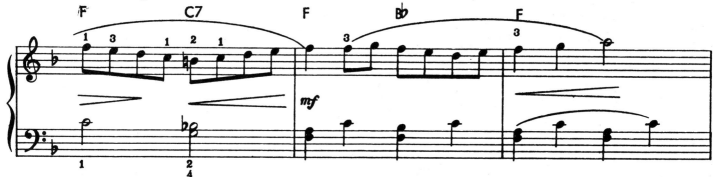

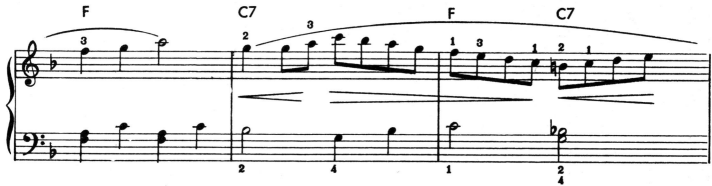

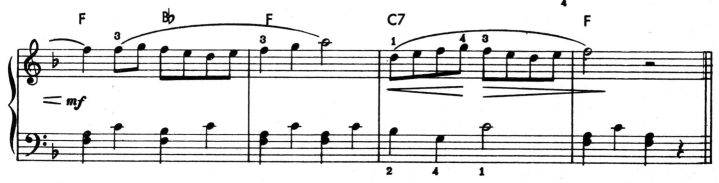

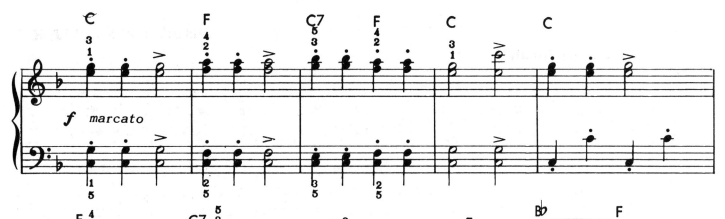

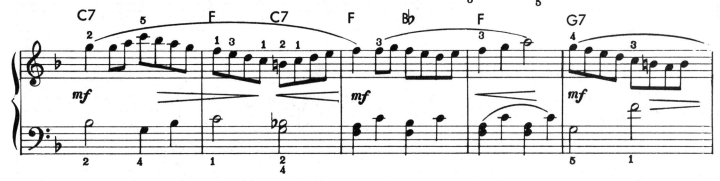

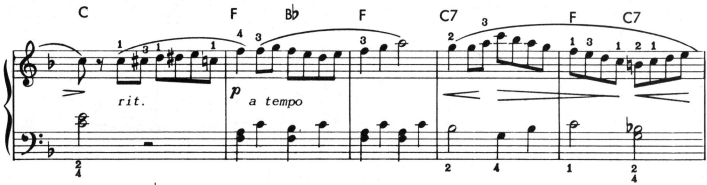

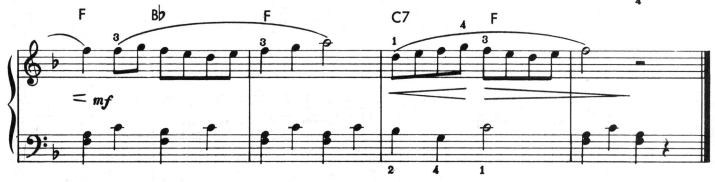

BASSO STACCATO

CARL CZERNY, Opus 599

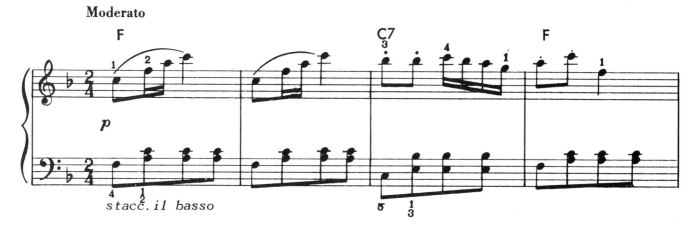

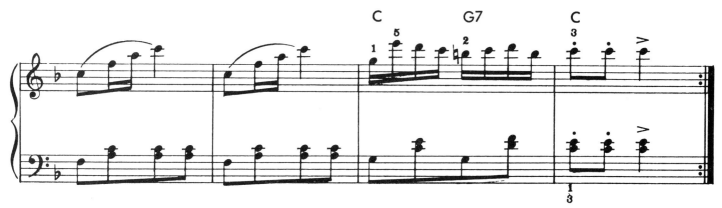

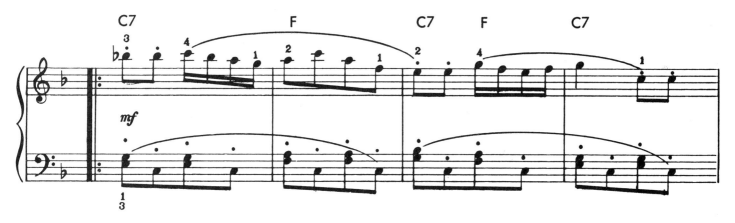

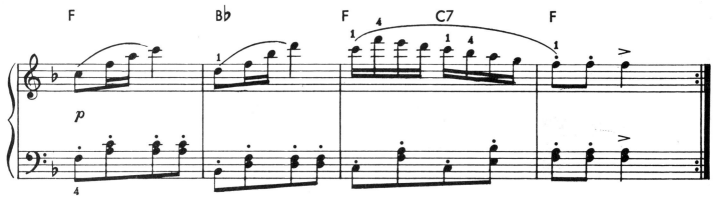

CANTABILE

CARL CZERNY, Opus 599

Andante (slowly)

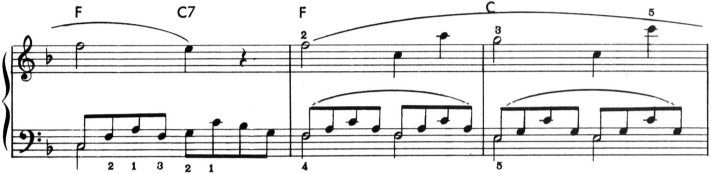

FRENCH FOLK TUNE

TRADITIONAL

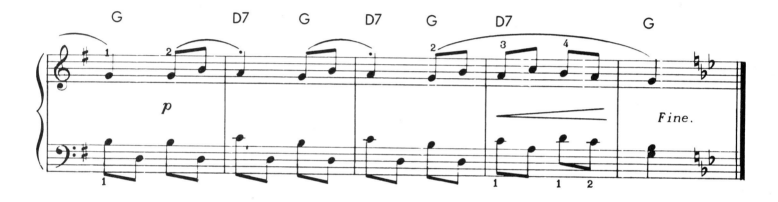

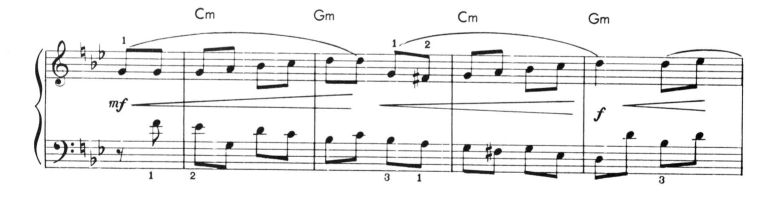

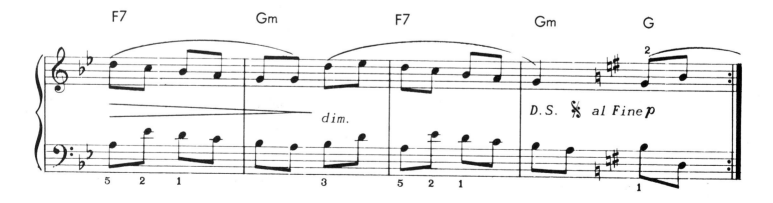

MARCH OF THE THREE KINGS

OLD FRENCH HYMN

Marcato moderato

TULIP

HEINRICH LICHNER, Opus 111, No. 4

Allegretto

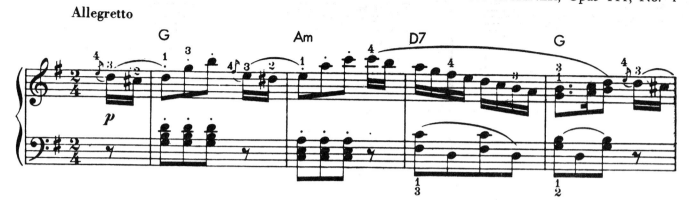

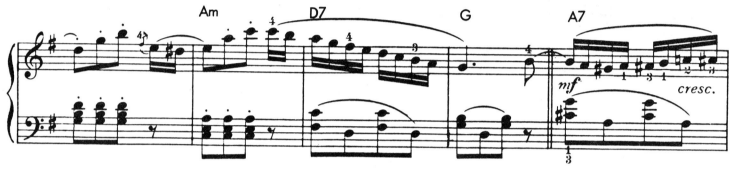

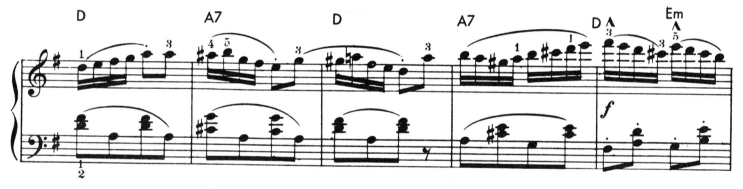

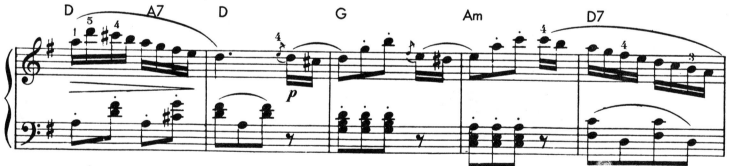

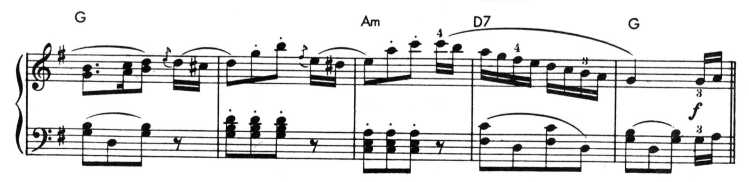

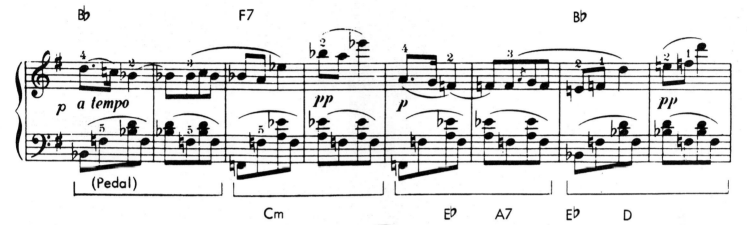

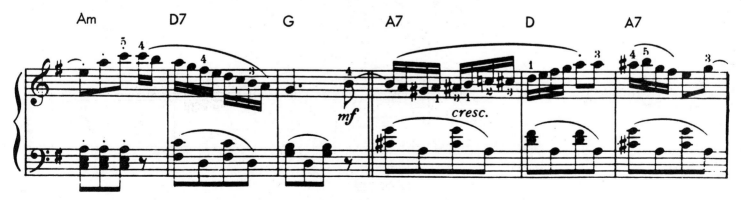

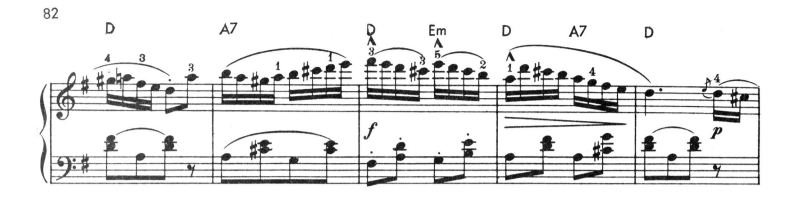

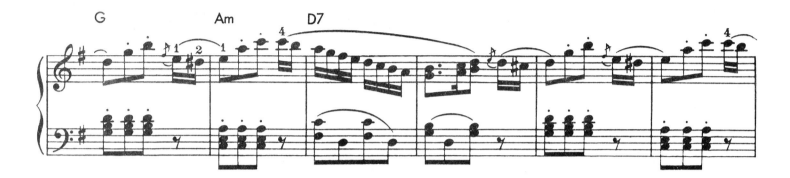

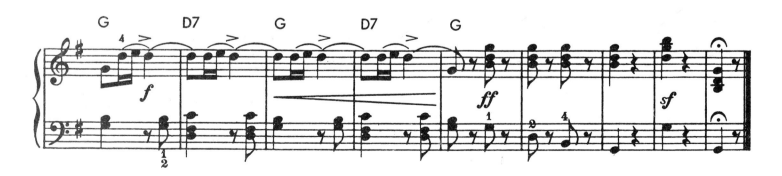

STARLIGHT WALTZ

Valse moderato

CHARLES S. BRAINARD

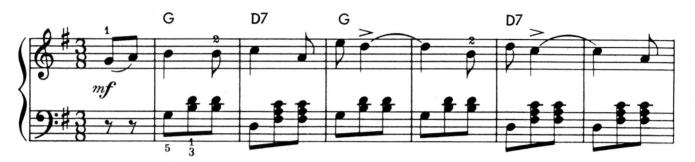

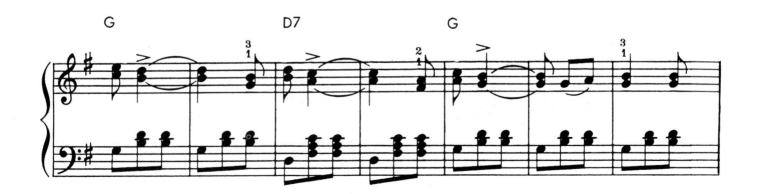

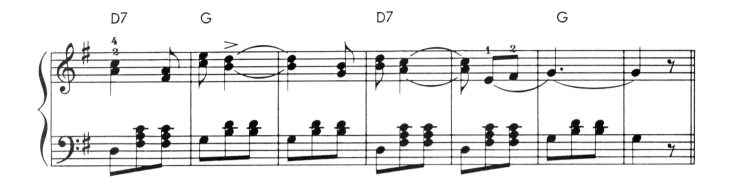

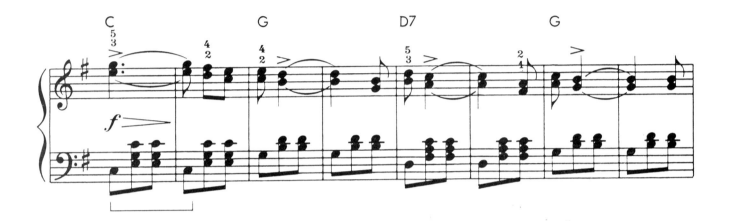

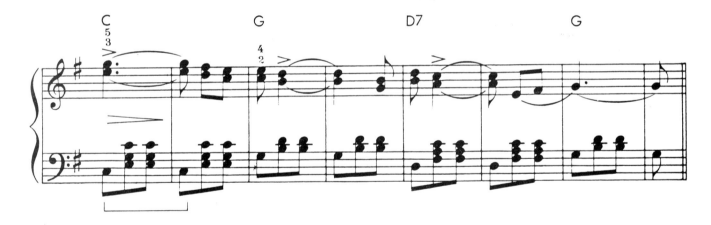

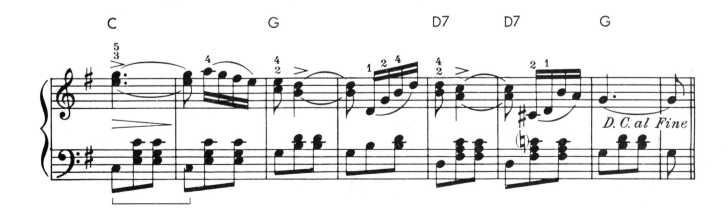

MINUET IN G

(MINUET No. 2)

LUDWIG VAN BEETHOVEN

Minuet moderato

TRIO

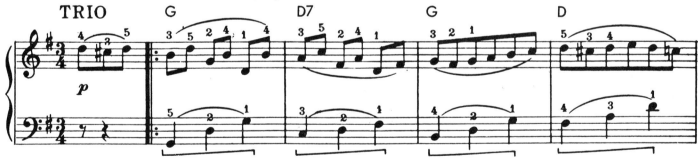

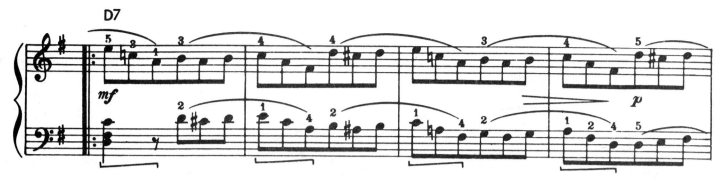

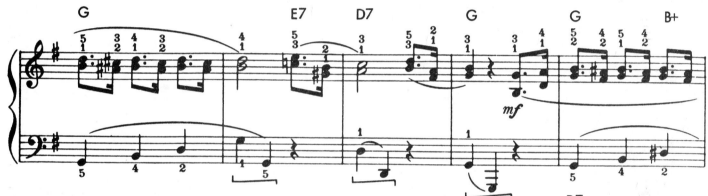

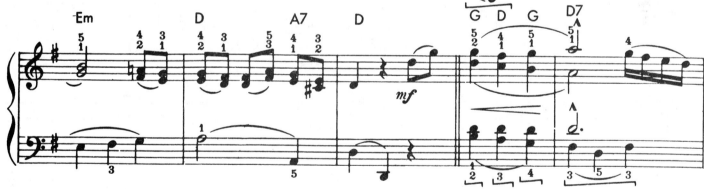

ANDANTE

BELA BARTOK

Andante (slowly)

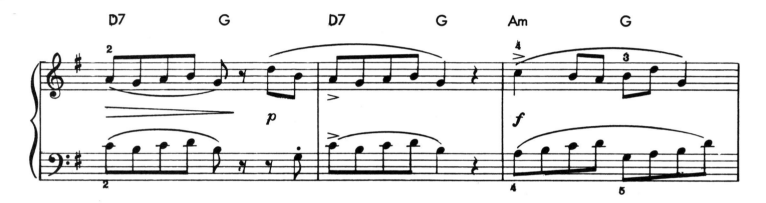

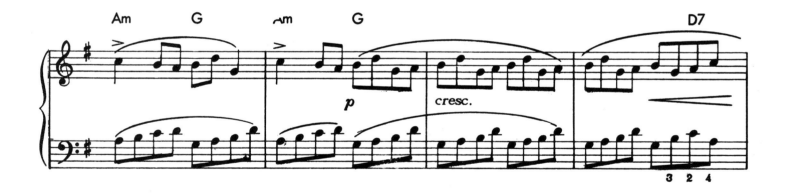

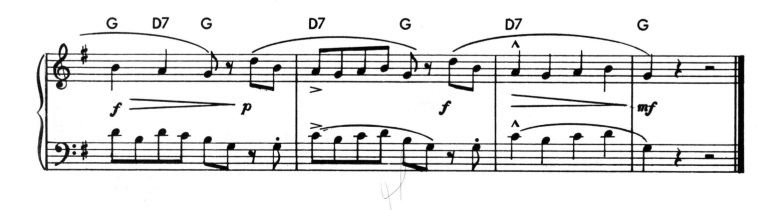

GERMAN DANCE

LUDWIG VAN BEETHOVEN

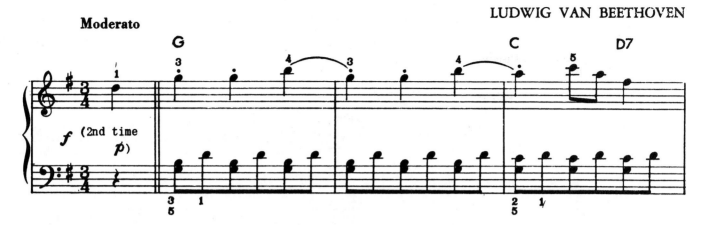

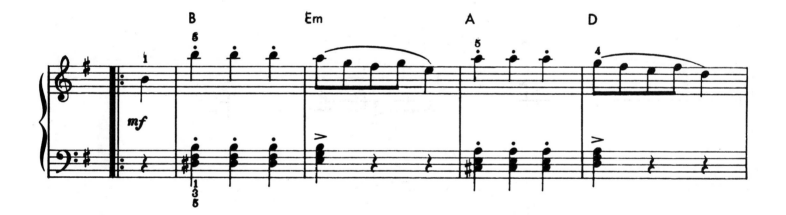

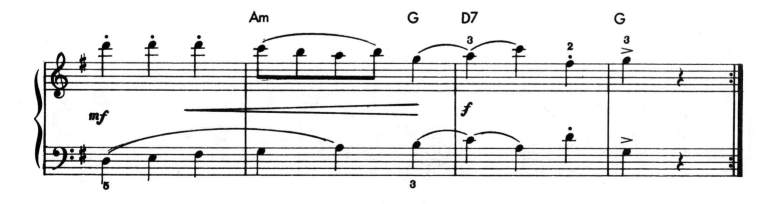

MINUET FROM SONATA
(OPUS 49, No. 2)

LUDWIG VAN BEETHOVEN

Minuet moderato

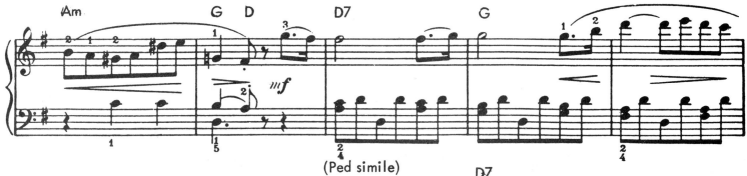

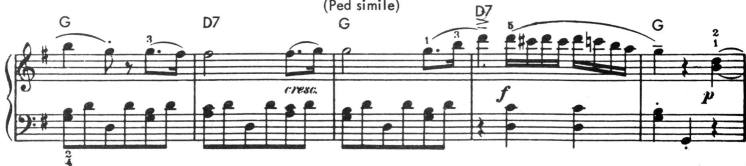

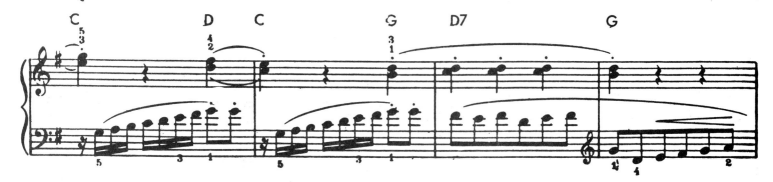

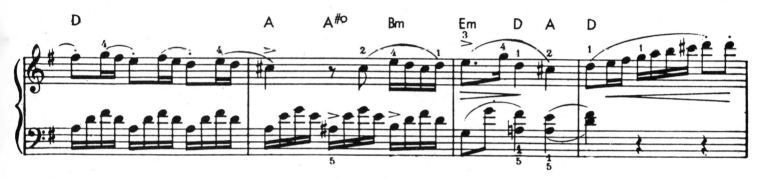

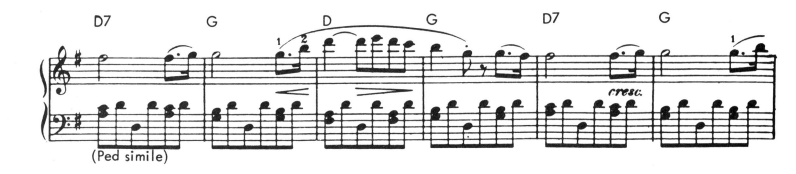

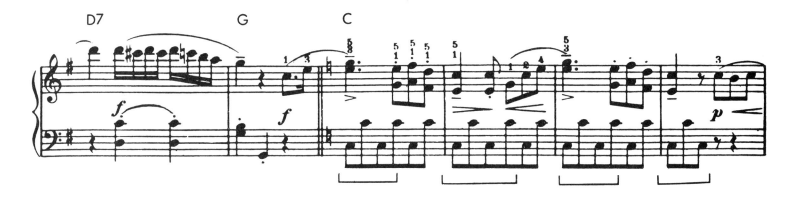

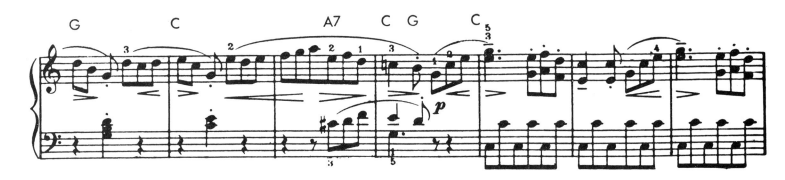

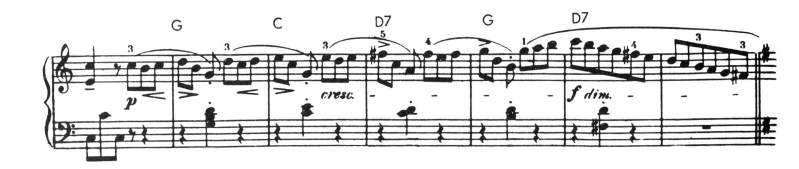

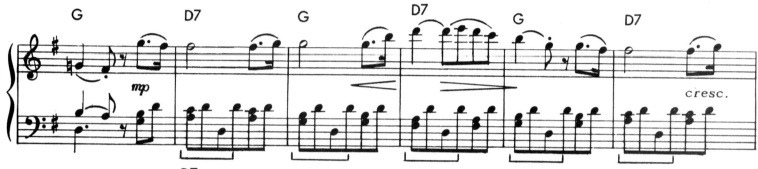

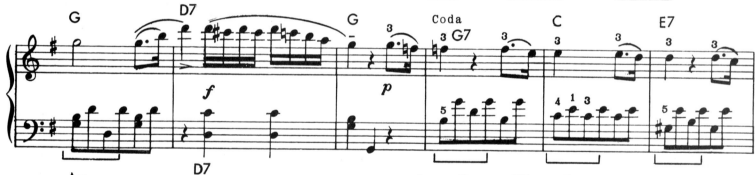

RONDO FROM SONATINA IN G

LOUIS KOEHLER, Opus 300

Allegretto

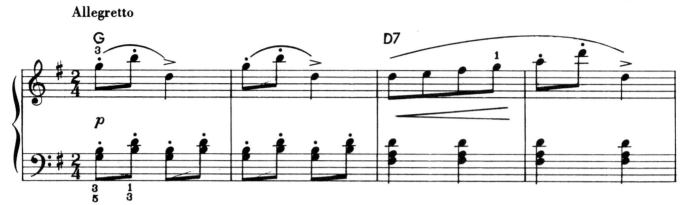

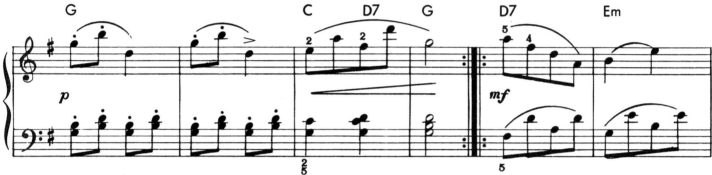

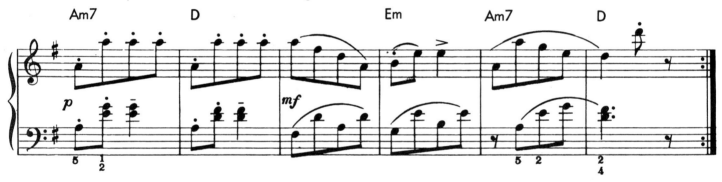

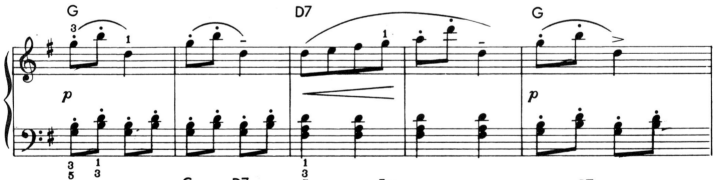

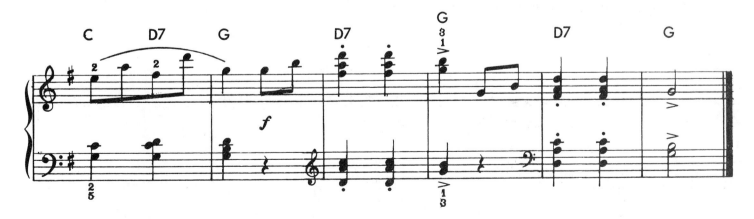

DANCING TWINS

DMITRI KABALEVSKY

Animato (lively)

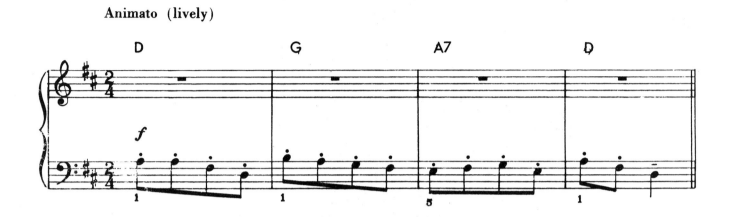

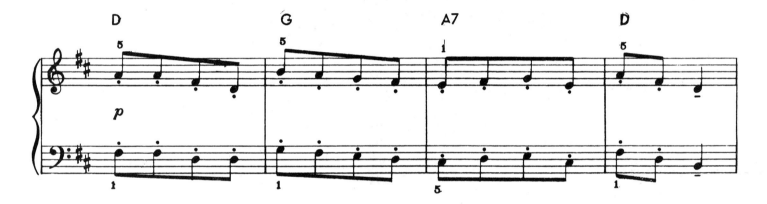

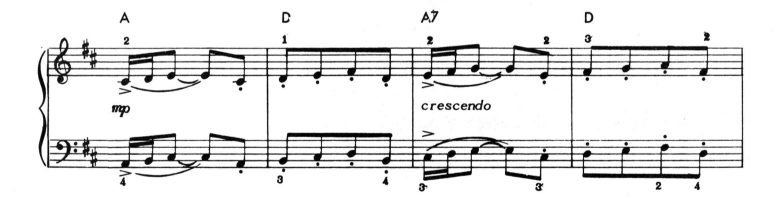

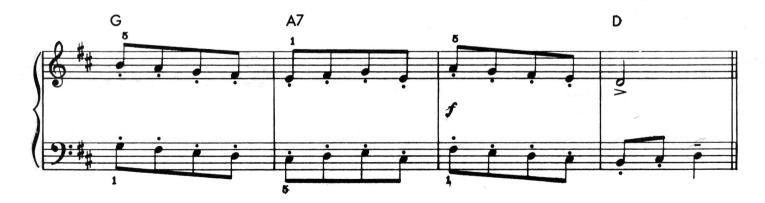

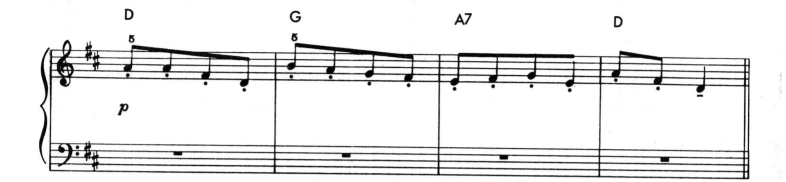

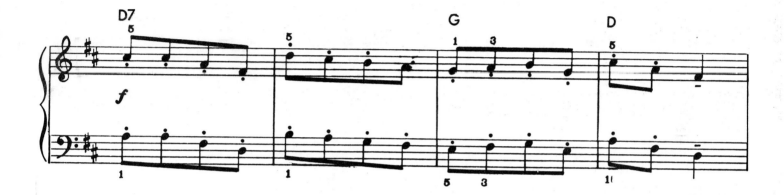

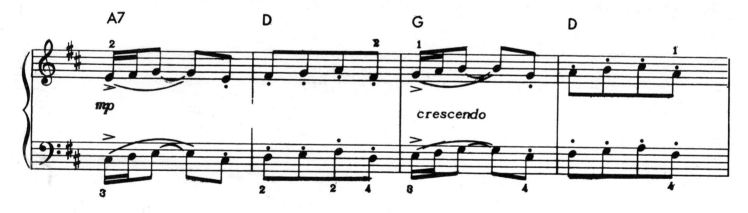

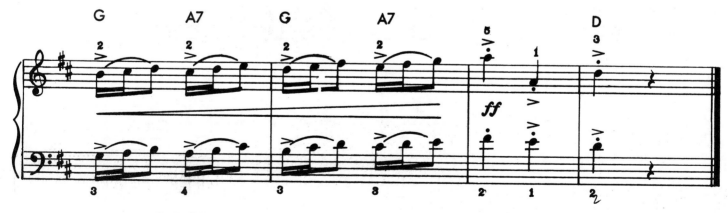

RONDO ALL TURCA

FRED BURGMUELLER, Opus 68

Allegretto

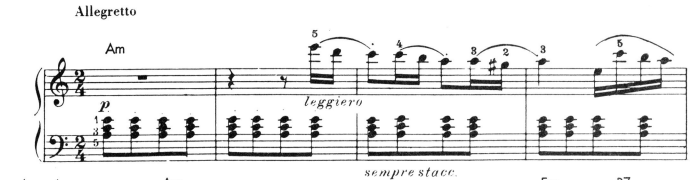

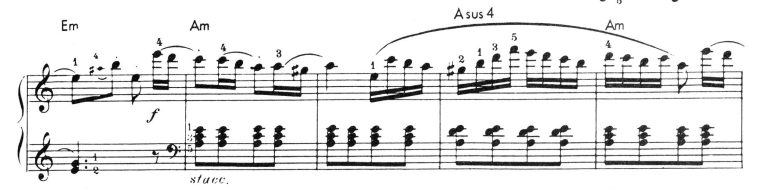

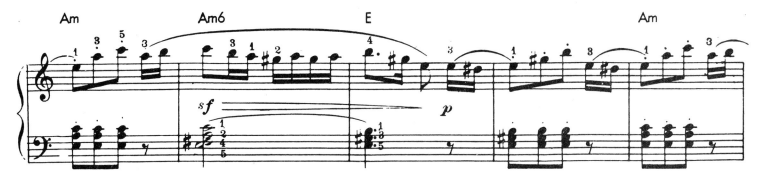

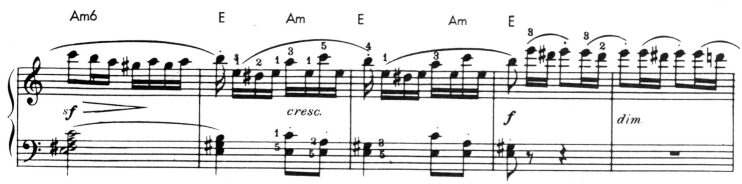

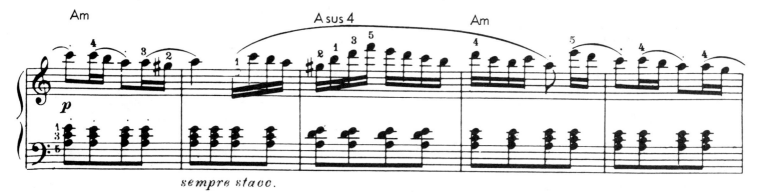

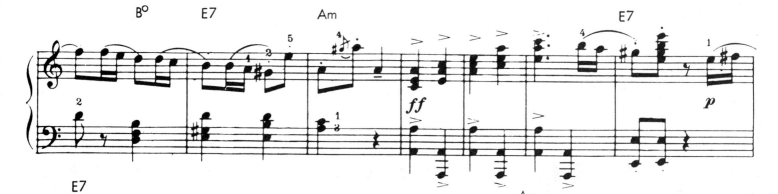

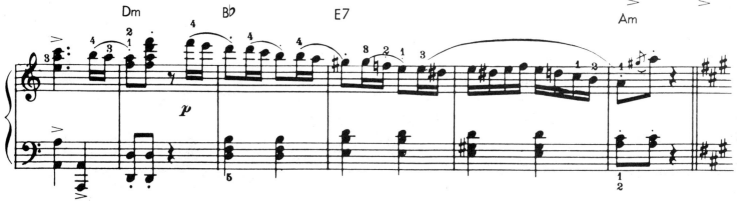

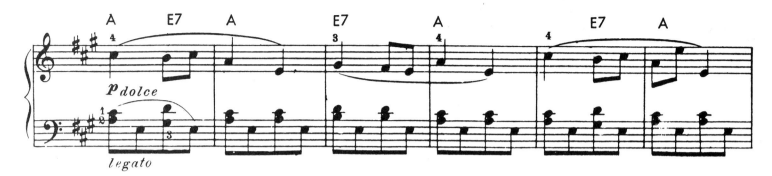

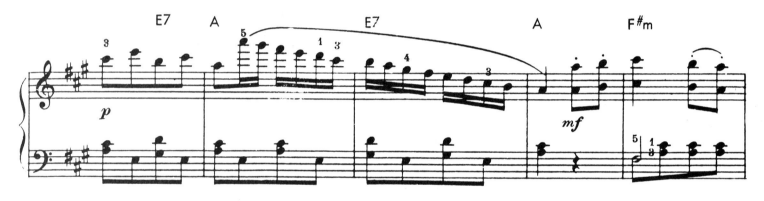

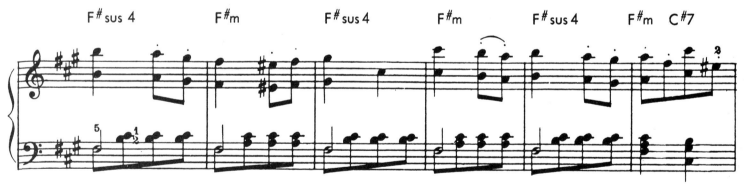

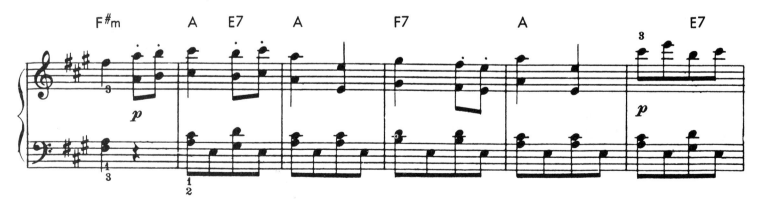

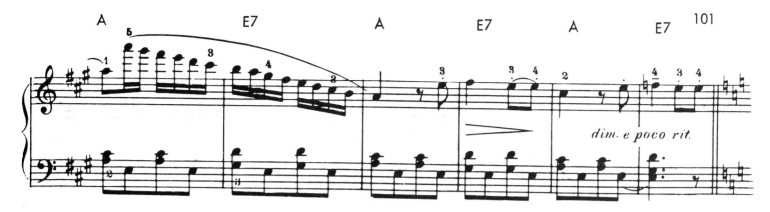

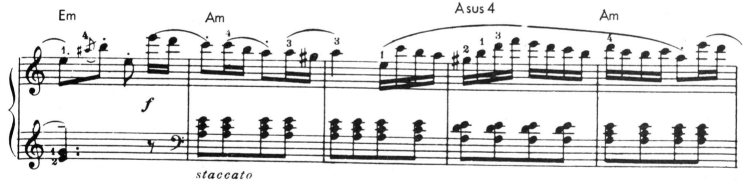

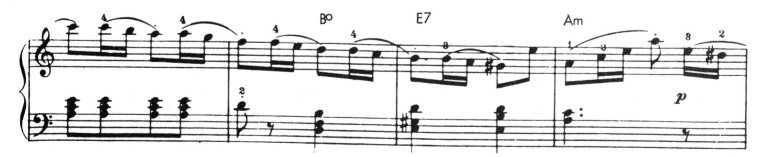

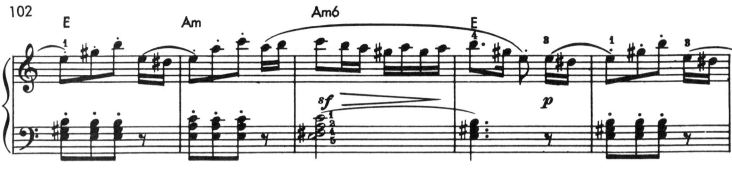

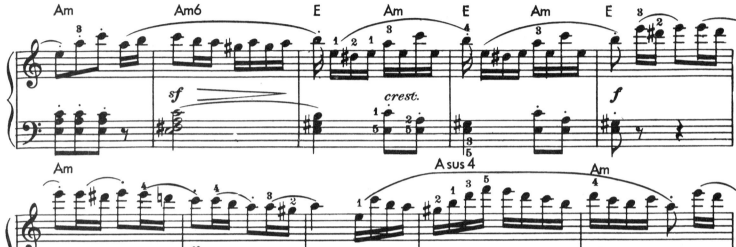

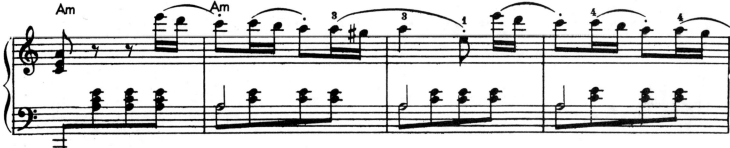

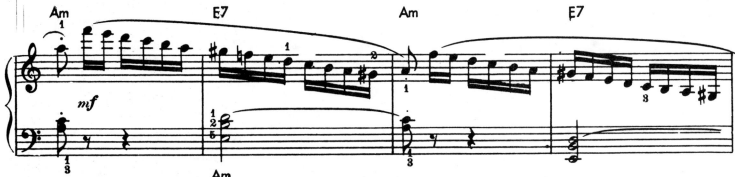

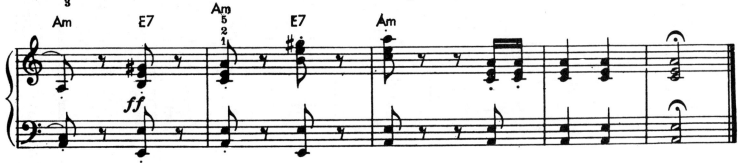

THE BEE AND THE CLOVER

ADAM GEIBEL

Allegro giocoso (playfully)

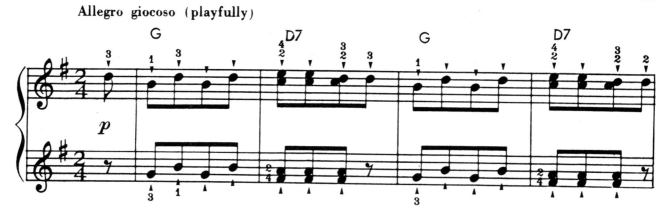

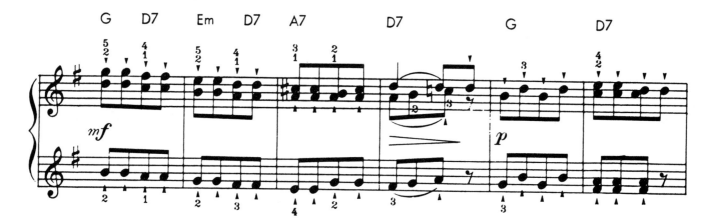

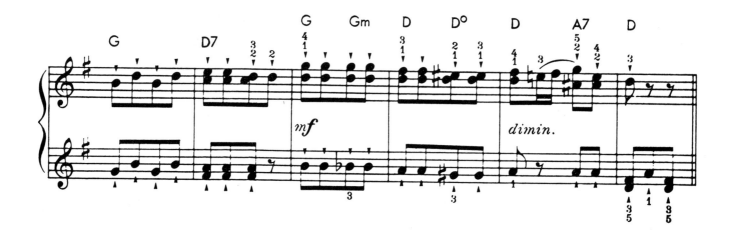

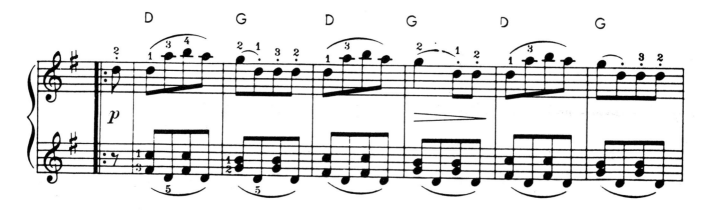

BLUE DANUBE WALTZ
(AN ORIGINAL STREABBOG ARRANGEMENT)

JOHANN STRAUSS

(ARRANGED BY LOUIS STREABBOG, Opus 86)

Valse moderato

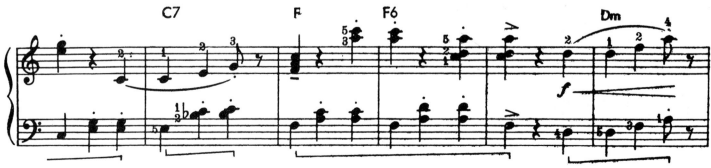

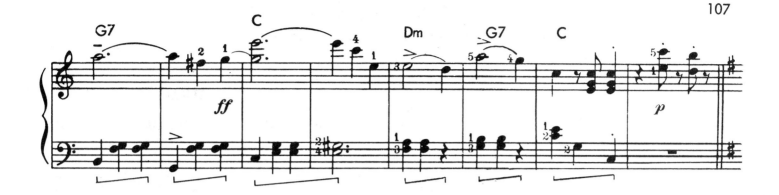

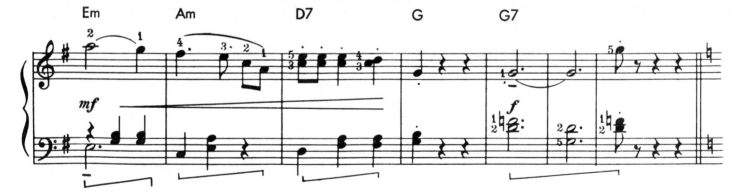

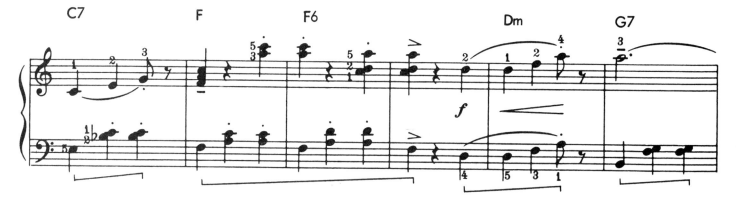

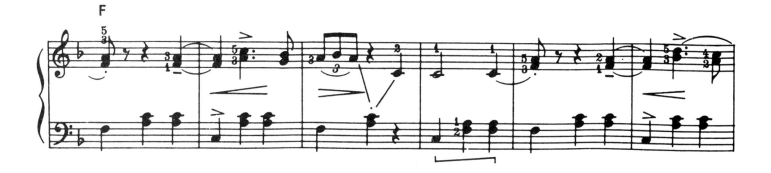

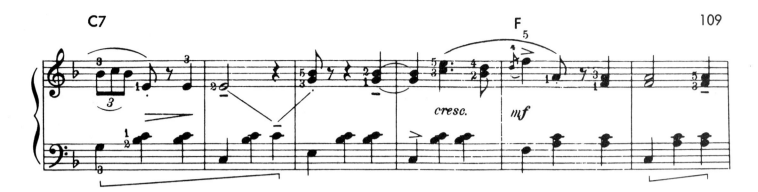

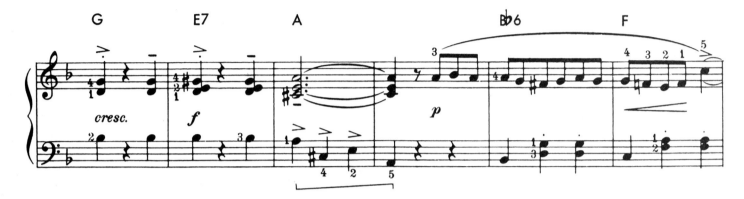

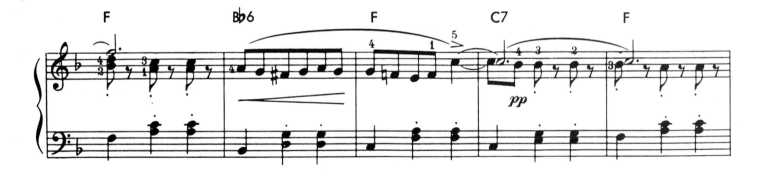

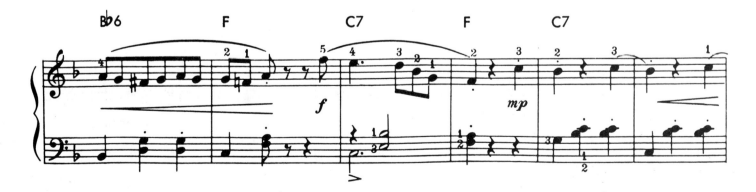

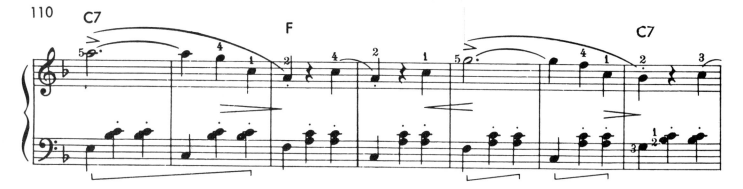

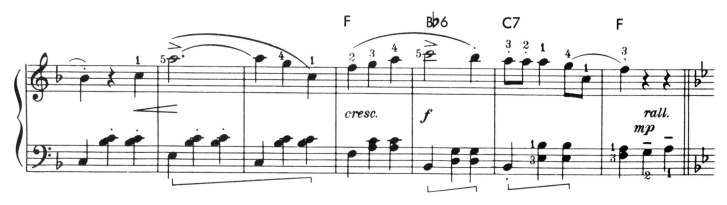

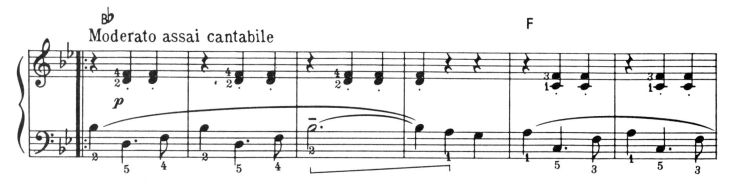

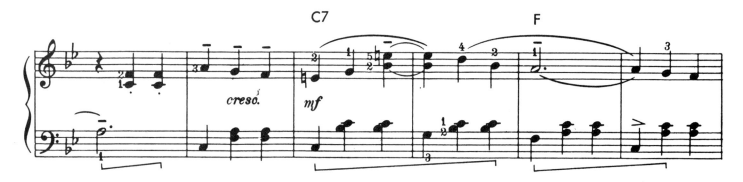

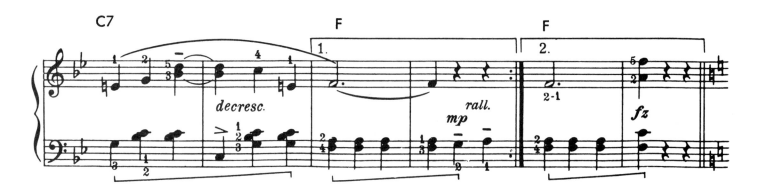

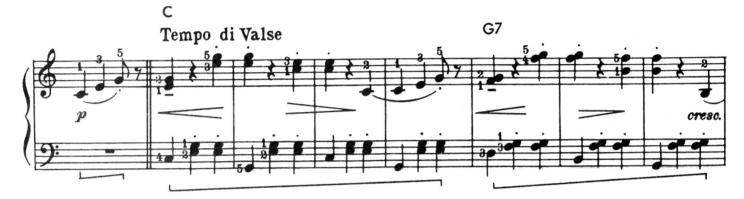

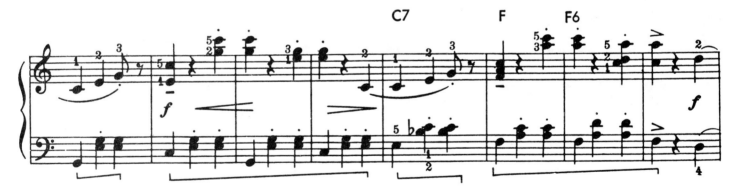

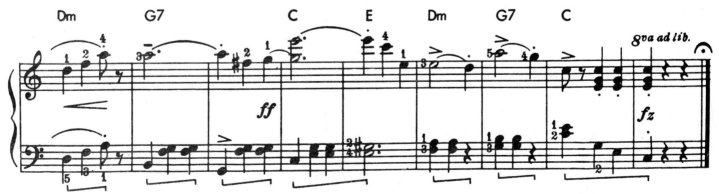

MINUET
(FROM "DON GIOVANI")

WOLFGANG AMADEUS MOZART

Moderato

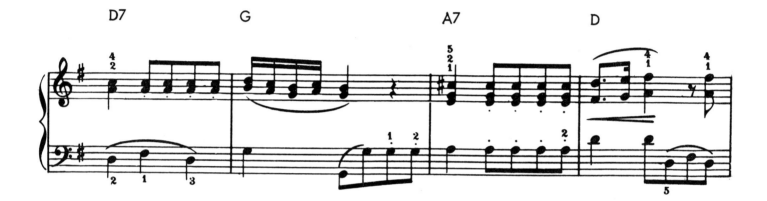

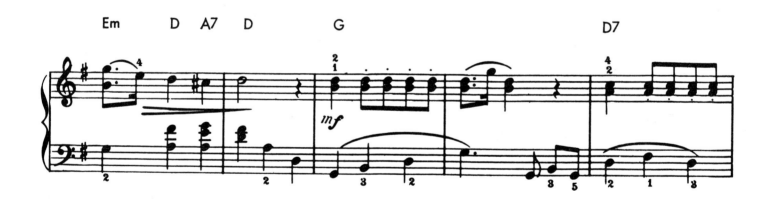

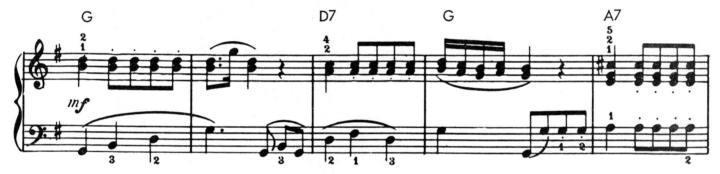

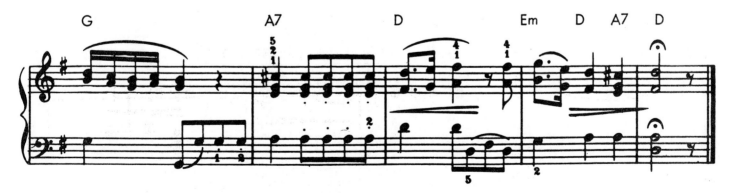

SONATINA

(PART 1)

Allegro moderato

ALBERT BIEHL, Opus 57, No. 1

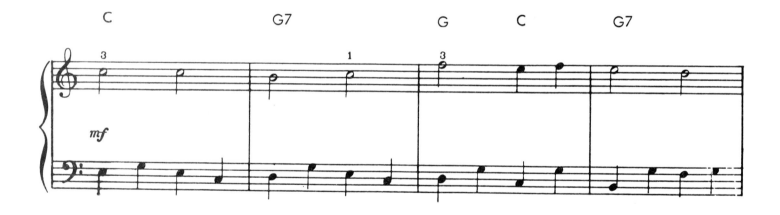

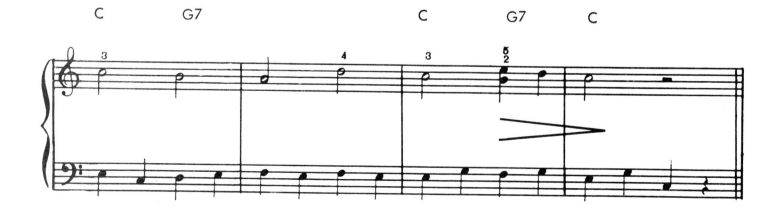

(PART 1)

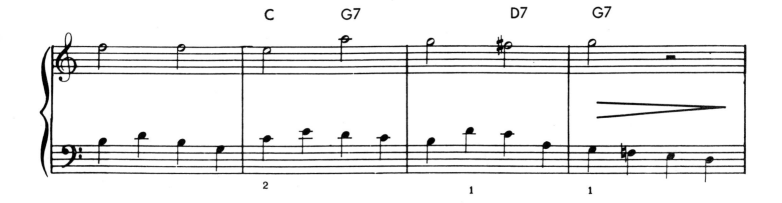

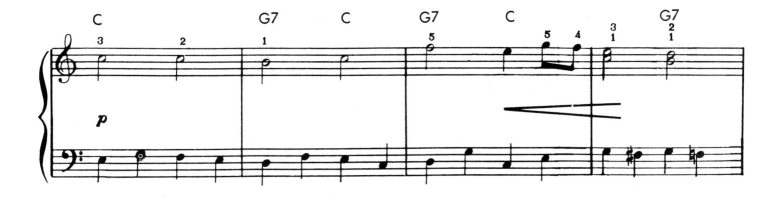

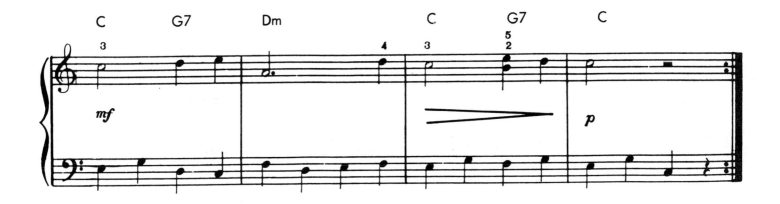

SONATINA
(PART 2 — RONDO)

ALBERT BIEHL, Opus 57, No. 1

Allegro grazioso (gracefully)

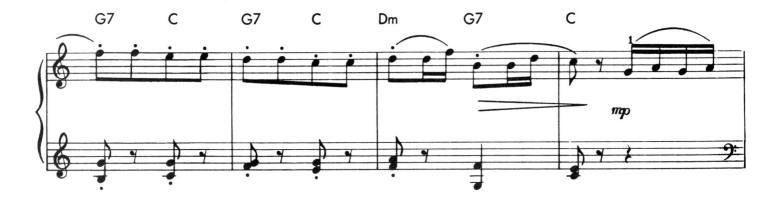

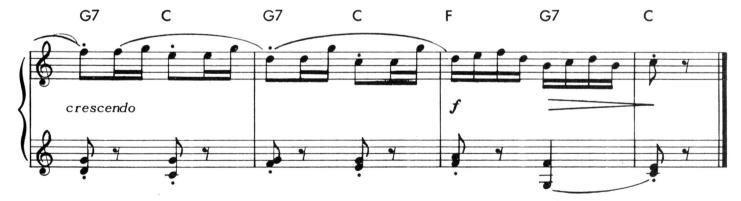

SONATINA No. 2
(PART 1)

JEAN LATOUR

Allegretto

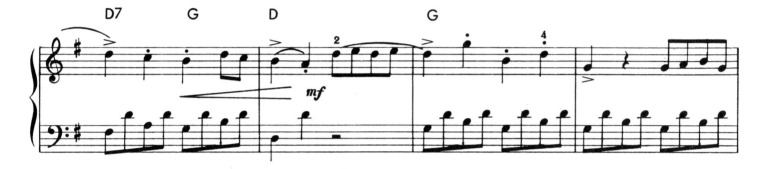

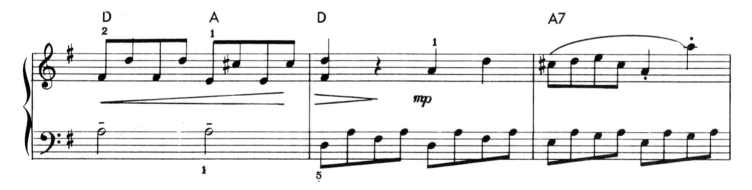

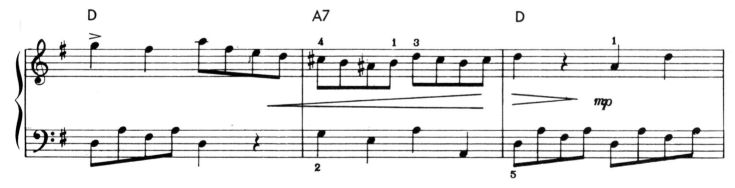

SONATINA

HEINRICH LICHNER

Allegro moderato

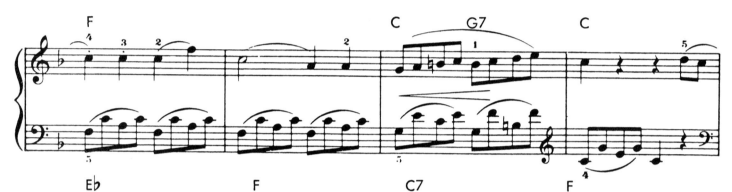

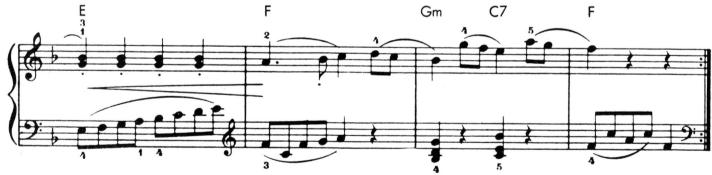

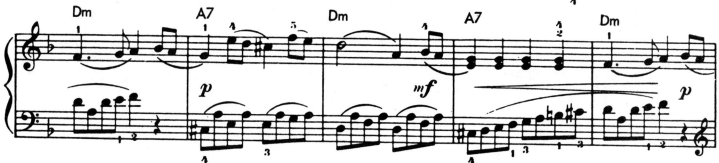

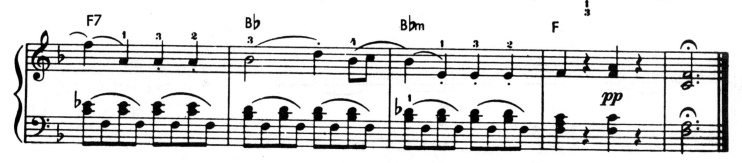

SONATINA

JAKOB SCHMITT

Moderato

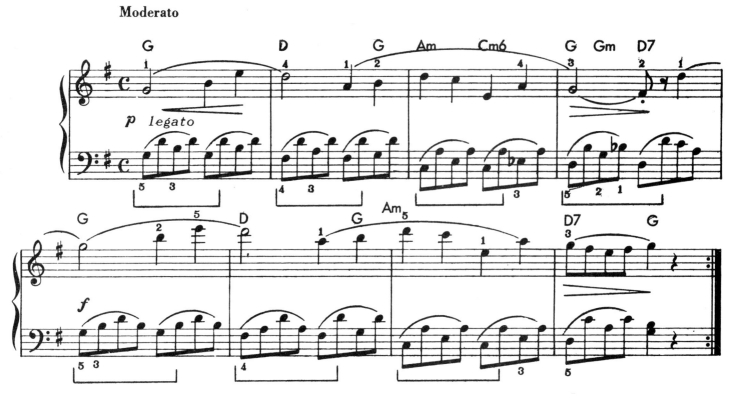

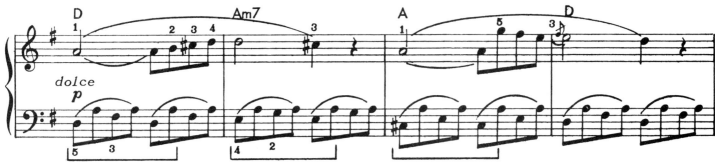

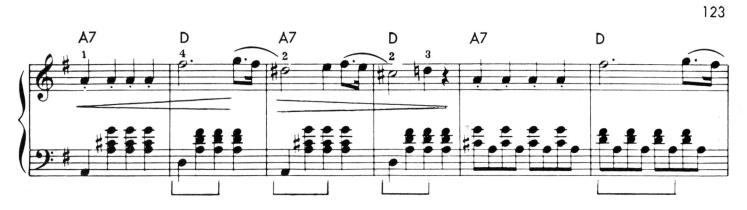

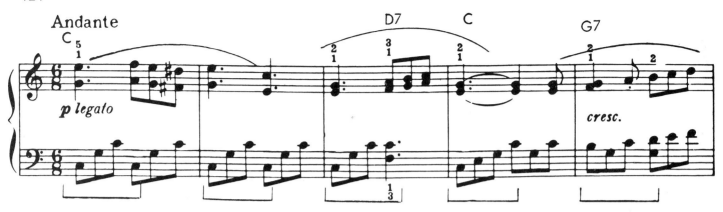

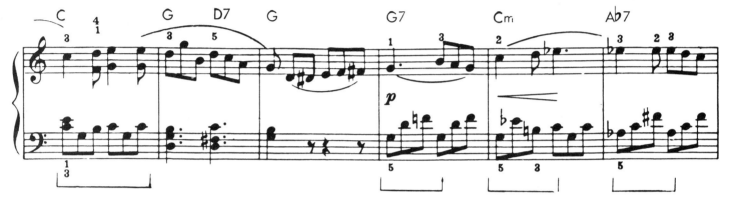

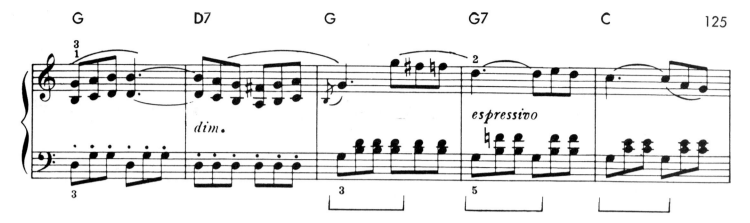

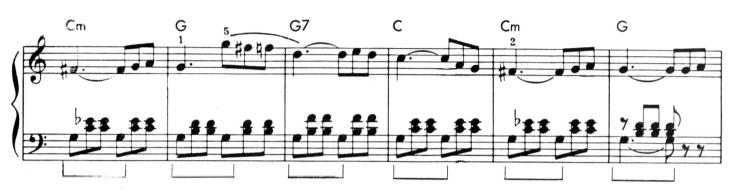

RONDO

Allegretto

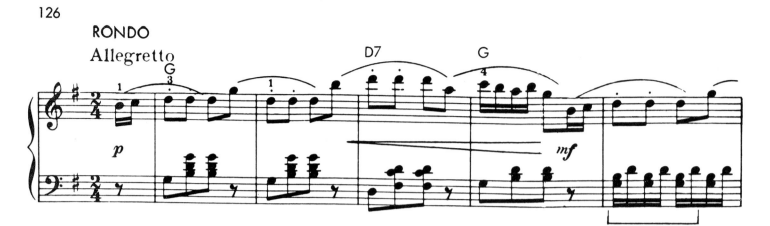

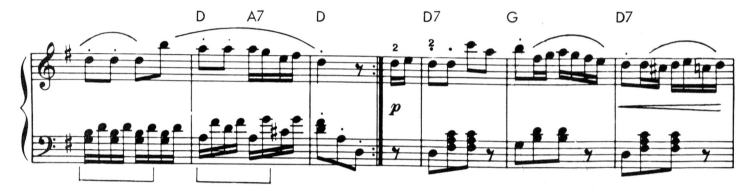

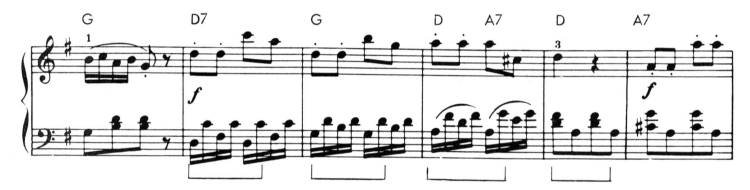

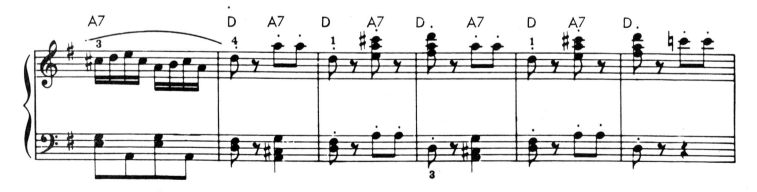

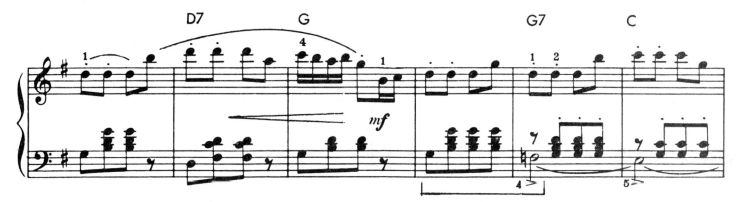

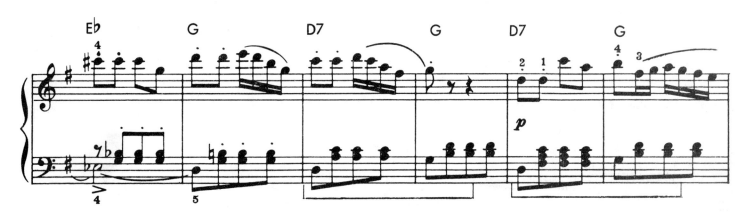

BOOGIE PIECE

STUART MONROE

Lively